Jura: Language and Landscape

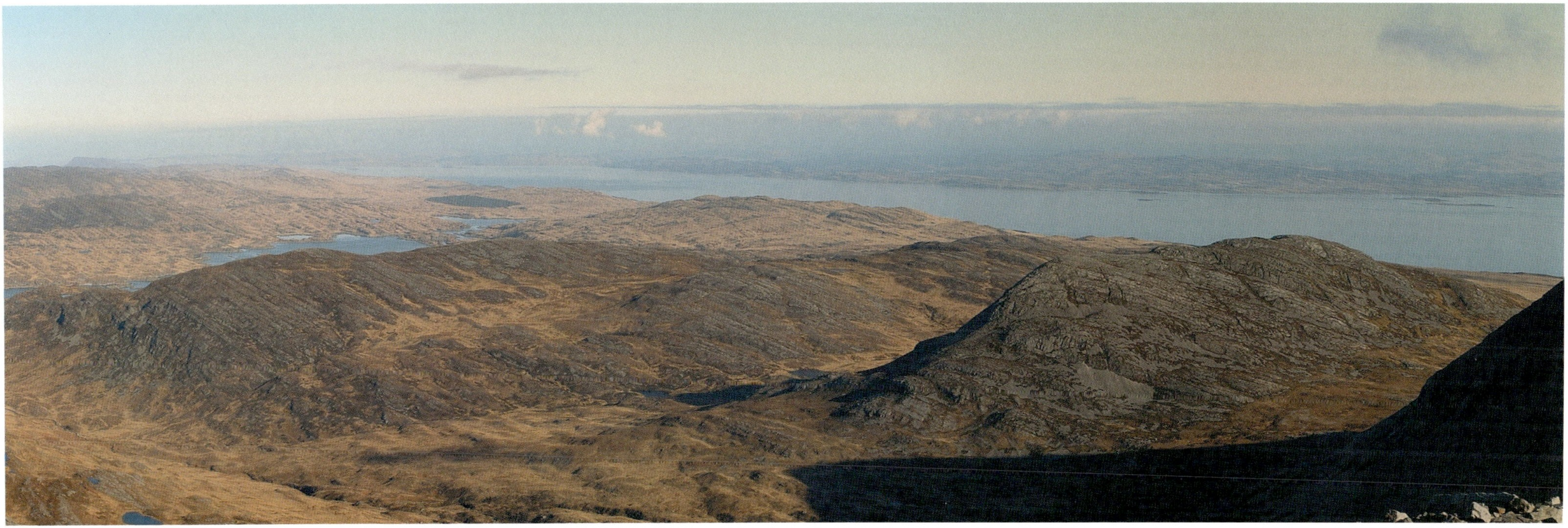

Gary McKay

Acknowledgements

This book, and the research underlying it, is the product of the support of many individuals and organisations. In advance I apologise to anyone I have forgotten. But to begin…The Lithgow Trust, The Catherine McKichan Trust, The Columba Centre of Islay, Inver, Ardfin, Jura Forest, Ruantallin, Ardlussa and Barnhill Estates on the Isle of Jura – and all their staff – as well as the Knockrome-Ardfarnal Common Grazing Community, the Fletchers of Persabus and Bealachruadh, Islay, Roger Eaton of the "Angie", the Jura Bus Company, Jura Stores – and last but not the least, the crew of the Jura Ferry who, though home-ported on Islay, have the "blessed island" in their rear-view mirror every time they return to Port Askaig.

The place name translations used in this book are based upon *Dwelly's Illustrated Gaelic to English Dictionary* which is considered to be the master work for the language.

The grid coordinates for each place are derived from the Ordnance Survey map *Jura and Scarba* (No.355 in the Explorer series) and are given in the standard form; easting grid numbers first and northing second.

Finally, the oral stories and related histories are based upon the Gaelic stories collected and translated by Robertson *Fada* [Tall Robertson], a beloved Jura minister of the early twentieth century. The written stories have been compared against current oral versions of the stories as well as against what written history exists to round them out. In most cases the oral relations are astonishingly accurate with only minor variations. Like fine antique furniture, these oral stories gain more lustre with each and every retelling by successive generations of *Diurach*.

Bibliography and Suggested Further Reading

Adomnan of Iona, *Life of St Columba*, tr. Richard Sharpe (1995)

Budge, Donald, *Jura an Island of Argyll* (1960)

Dwelly, Edward, *Dwelly's Illustrated Gaelic to English Dictionary* (1901)

Martin, Martin, *A Description of the Western Islands of Scotland* (1703)

Mercer, John, *Hebridean Islands; Colonsay, Gigha, Jura* (1974).

Severin, Tim, *The Brendan Voyage* (1978)

Watson, W.J., *History of the Celtic Place-Names of Scotland* (1926)

Wright, Gordon, and Tait, Norman, *The Isle of Jura; Images from the Past* (1994)

Wright, Gordon, and Tait, Norman, *The Isle of Jura; Memories from the Past* (1998)

Youngson, Peter, *Ancient Hebridean Tales of Jura*, (1985)

Youngson, Peter, *Jura: Island of Deer*, (2001)

First published 2005
by House of Lochar in collaboration with
The Feolin Study Centre, Isle of Jura

Text and photographs © 2005 Gary McKay

British Cataloguing in Publication Data
A catalogue record for this book is available
from the British Library

ISBN 1 899863 39 7

Printed in Great Britain by Amadeus Press, Cleckheaton

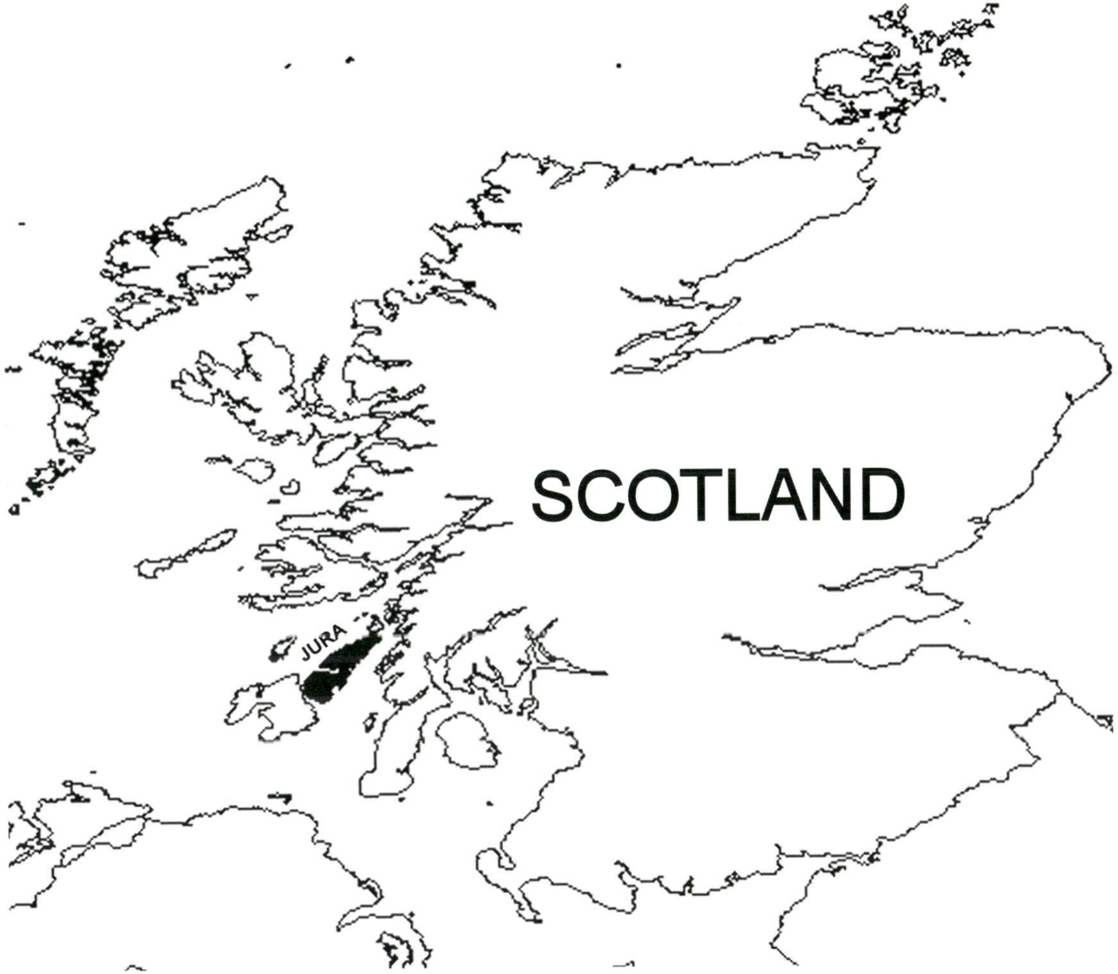

SCOTLAND

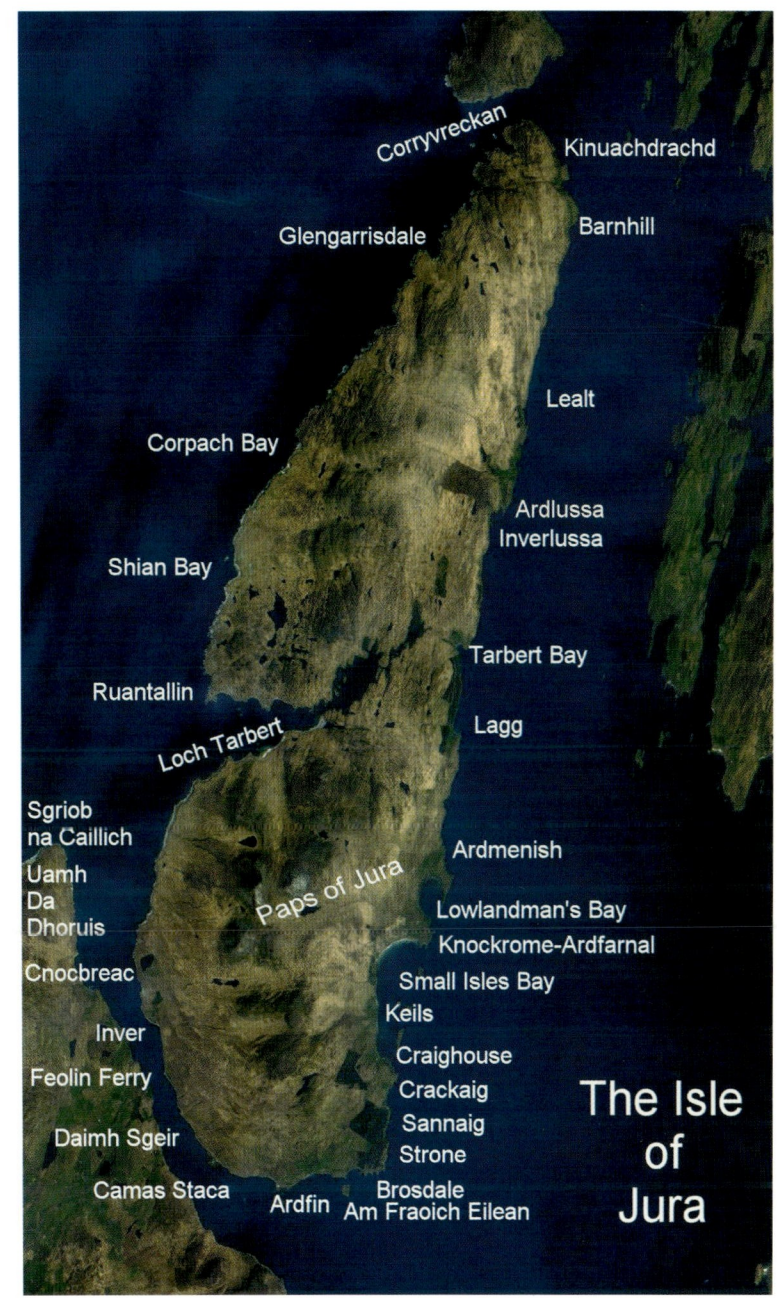

The Isle
of
Jura

Corryvreckan
Kinuachdrachd
Glengarrisdale
Barnhill
Lealt
Corpach Bay
Ardlussa
Inverlussa
Shian Bay
Tarbert Bay
Ruantallin
Lagg
Loch Tarbert
Sgriob
na Caillich
Ardmenish
Uamh
Da
Dhoruis
Paps of Jura
Lowlandman's Bay
Knockrome-Ardfarnal
Cnocbreac
Small Isles Bay
Keils
Inver
Craighouse
Feolin Ferry
Crackaig
Sannaig
Daimh Sgeir
Strone
Camas Staca
Brosdale
Ardfin
Am Fraoich Eilean

JURA

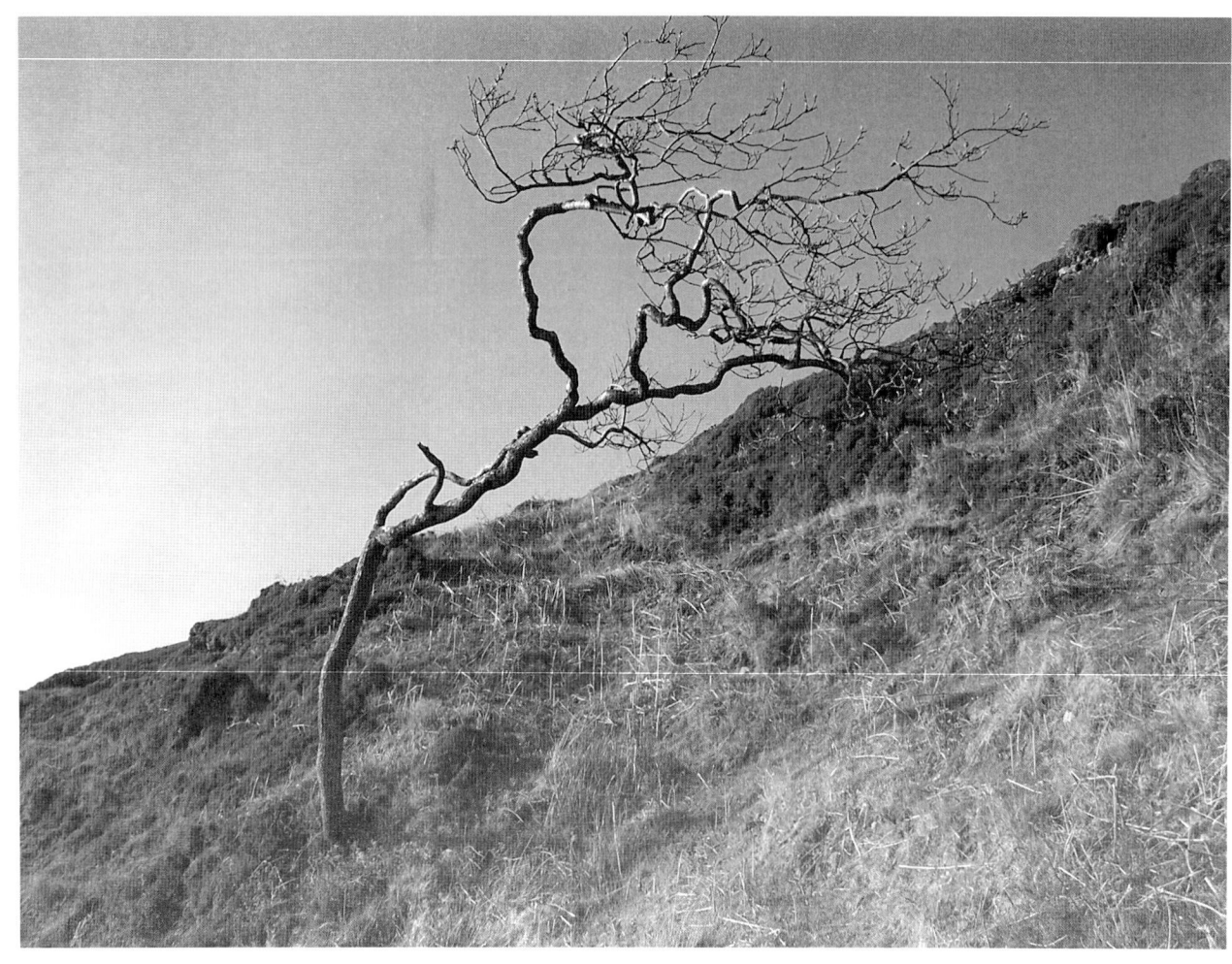

Tree at McDougall's Bay

Introduction

The Isle of Jura has perhaps suffered more at the hands of indiscriminate and perfunctory historians and writers than any other place in Scotland. Described variously throughout history as "wild", "rugged" and "inhospitable", or more recently as "Europe's last great wilderness", the island has also endured the ignominy of governmental apathy with the dubious accolade of being the only major island in the Hebrides not to have a direct mainland ferry service.

But, enough of the typical commentary concerning Jura, for now like Cervantes' literary hero, Don Quixote, I shall joust at windmills.

The very word Jura, or *Diura* in the Gaelic language, is a cognate word, meaning that it appears in several languages, even in the harsh language of English; it means "durable, tough or resilient". The word appears in the Jura Mountains of France, and even further beyond in Bulgaria. I like to think of the word as yet another almost forgotten piece of linguistic flotsam marking the path and passing of the Celtic civilisation –

whatever that may be, since even that is argued over by academics like crows upon a misbegotten scrap of stale bread. I also like to think that it is a word that describes perfectly the people of Jura – durable and resilient, but with a greater grace and dignity than may be found in the most cosmopolitan of places.

This is a book that hopes to do something very simple and straightforward. The intent is for the author to "get out of the way" and let Jura speak for herself. Her native children who spoke the Gaelic dialect of *Diurach* [natives of Jura] are virtually gone; all that is left are the place names and the oral stories contained in a few minor manuscripts or in the gently declining memories of some current islanders.

Yet, this paucity of information lends itself to a greater sense of dignity about the island's role in history. From being a meeting place of saints and holy men, who ostensibly used the island as a retreat for contemplation, to accommodating that most famous of commentators on political oppression, George Orwell, the Isle of Jura's

timeless role as a place of serenity is undeniable.

I have tried to capture this serenity and dignity by reconnecting original Gaelic stories to their landscapes for the first time, thus allowing readers to make their own judgements. The photographs themselves are the result of a three-year long effort to photograph all the places on Jura with Gaelic names – and to translate the names as well – of which a very few were exhibited during 2004. Over 46,000 photographs were captured from over 90,000 acres and 115 miles of coastline; innumerable broken walking sticks, worn-out boots and peat-stained trousers were gained along the way.

My own interpretation of Jura is not of a wild, rugged place, but of an island that is somnambulant, that is to say merely slumbering, bemusedly ignoring man's vanities, but still, missing the sound of her "children" speaking the Gaelic, the language that describes her so well.

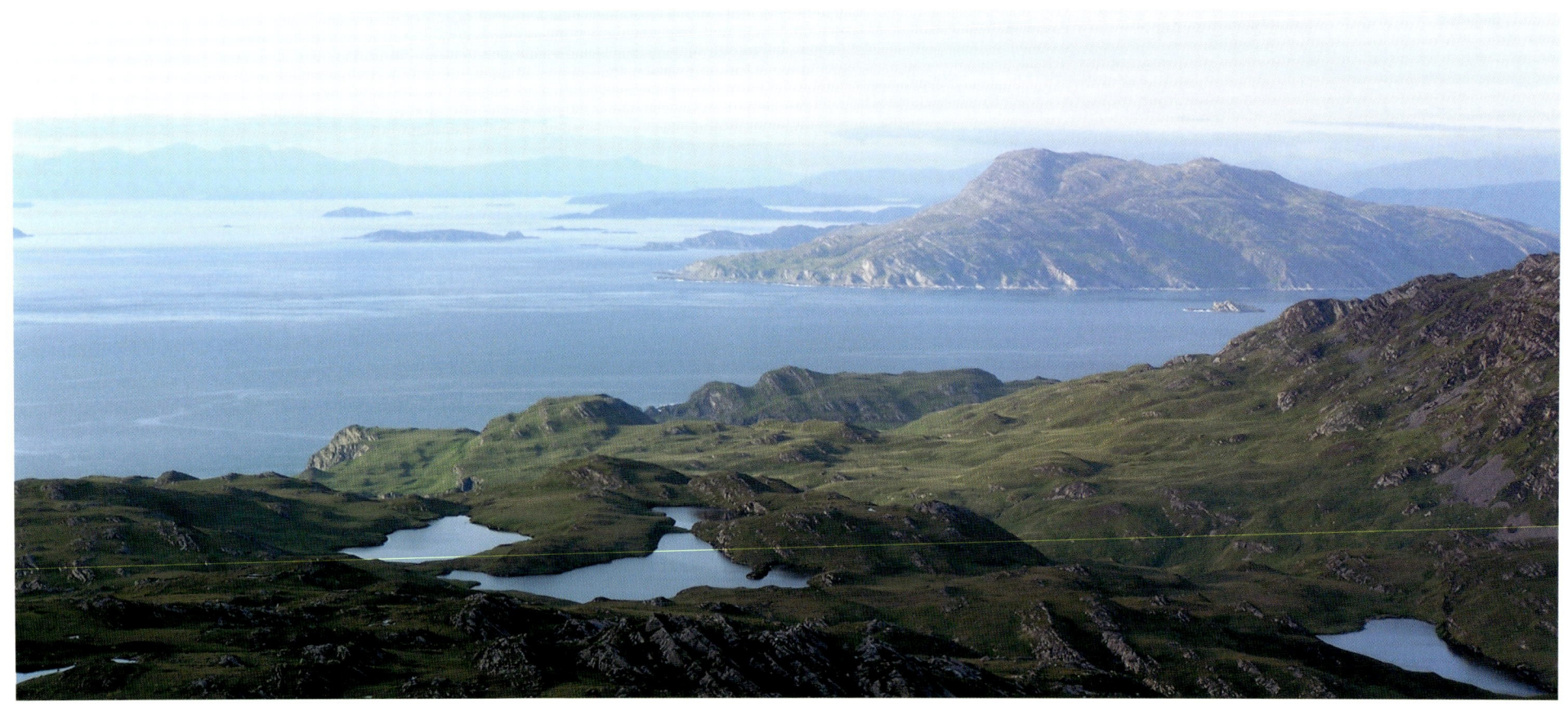

The view from *Beinn Bhreac* across the *Lochana Tana* to an unusually calm *Corryvreckan*. The mountain-island of *Scarba* looms above the normally turbid stretch of water.

Corryvreckan

The great trough of broken water

The physical feature that made Jura famous in early history, along with the Paps of Jura of course, is the Corryvreckan (NM 6950 0150). While much romantic history has been written about this maritime wonder, the truth is much more wonderful than the fiction. Early histories of the Irish Sea and Western Scotland refer to a *Coire Bhreacan* [region of extreme sea turbulence] lying off the north-north-east coast of Ireland, and it can be seen that the term was a transfer Gaelic place name employed whenever such maritime features were observed. In Jura's case, wonderful local legends exist about Danish or Norwegian princes with the name Brecan, struggling against the all-consuming sea to prove their love for some princess held by an unyielding father-king. And yet, it is a pity that the truth presented by the Gaelic language is not more widely known, for it is a magnificent term for a truly awe-inspiring natural feature, this great trough of broken water. In this spirit, here is a little known story, which mirrors the tales of Brecan, about how some now-forgotten *Díurachs* [natives of Jura] tested the powers of the Corryvreckan. It must be remembered that when the Isle of Scarba was inhabited by fishermen and shepherds travel across the gulf would have been a regular necessity.

An attempt was made once to ascertain what kind of rope would hold a boat against the currents and whirlpools of the Corryvreckan. The intrepid mariner made all sorts of ropes from all types of materials such as hemp, horsehair, and wool. When the seaman cast out his anchors into the gulf, he found the best rope was made of wool and concluded that a hawser made of wool would withstand the strain. Unfortunately, the seaman had too much faith in his own ingenuity, for the rope of wool frayed before the tidal rush of the gulf subsided, thus ending the life of the mariner and his loyal crewman.

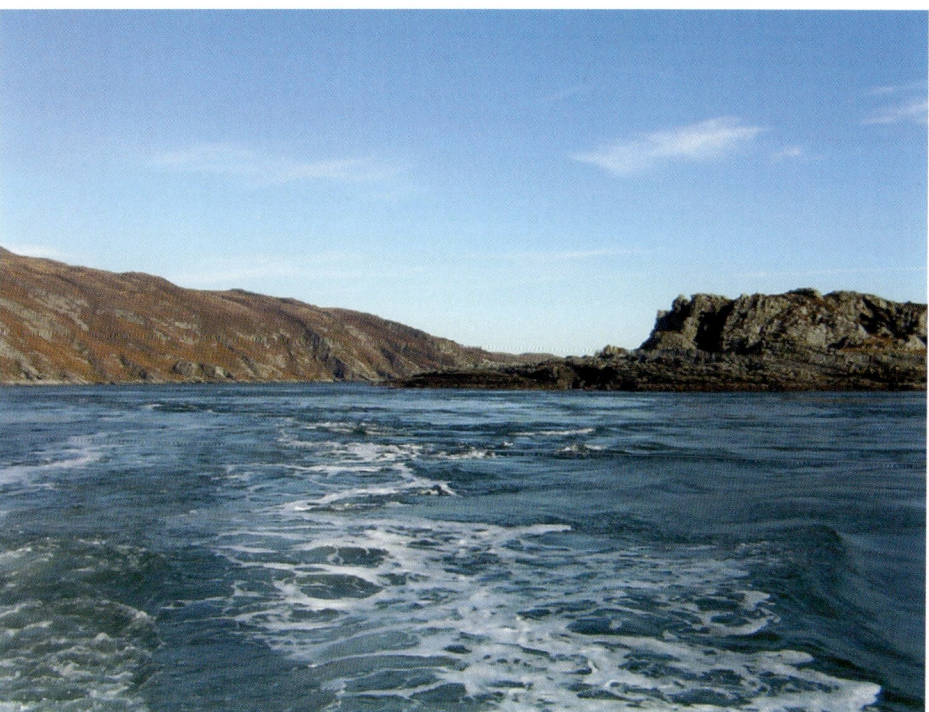

Barnhill

Cnoc an t-Sabhail *or Hill of the barn*

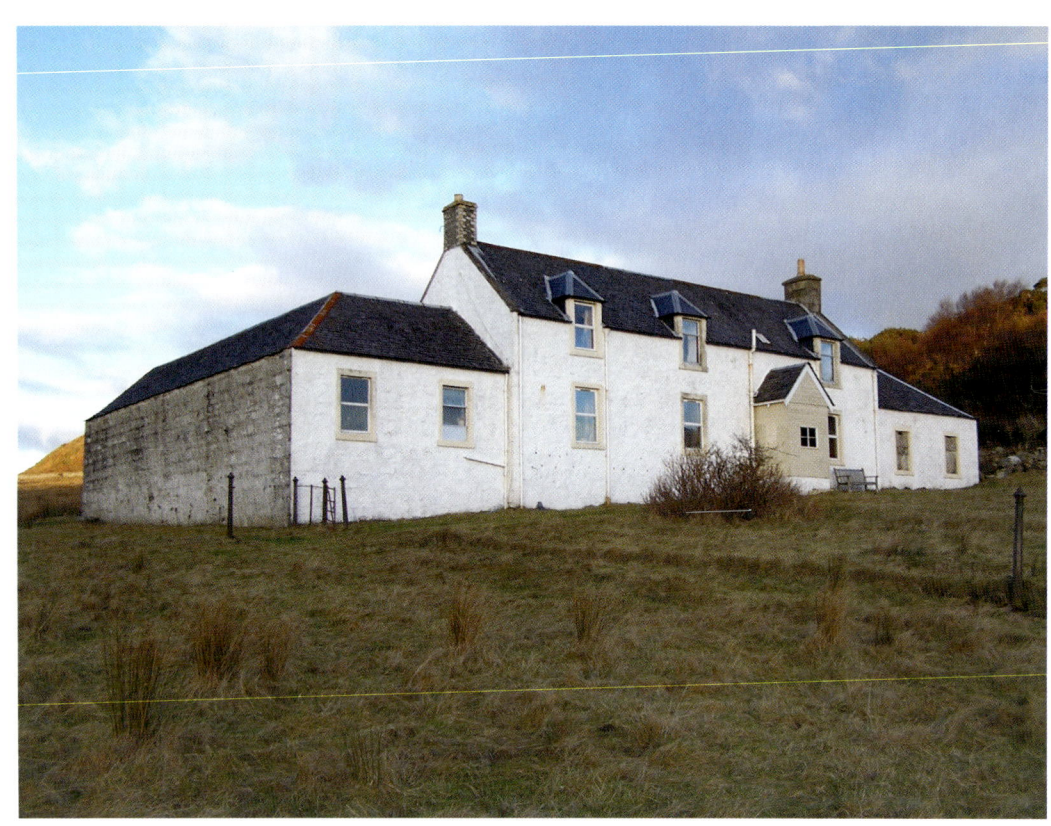

Barnhill (NR 7050 9710) is probably the most famous house or place on Jura, simply because George Orwell wrote the greatest part of his novel *1984* there, completing the first draft during 1947. The landscape around Barnhill contains many surprises, including the "lost" settlement of Troag, or Troig, which is not so lost if one consults early maps, the mystery of Con Tom with its standing stones, and the stunning view towards Scotland's ancient kingdom of Alba. But you have to really want to get to Barnhill to enjoy all this, as Orwell said himself in this oft-quoted quip: "It's in an extremely un-get-atable place, but it's a nice house…"

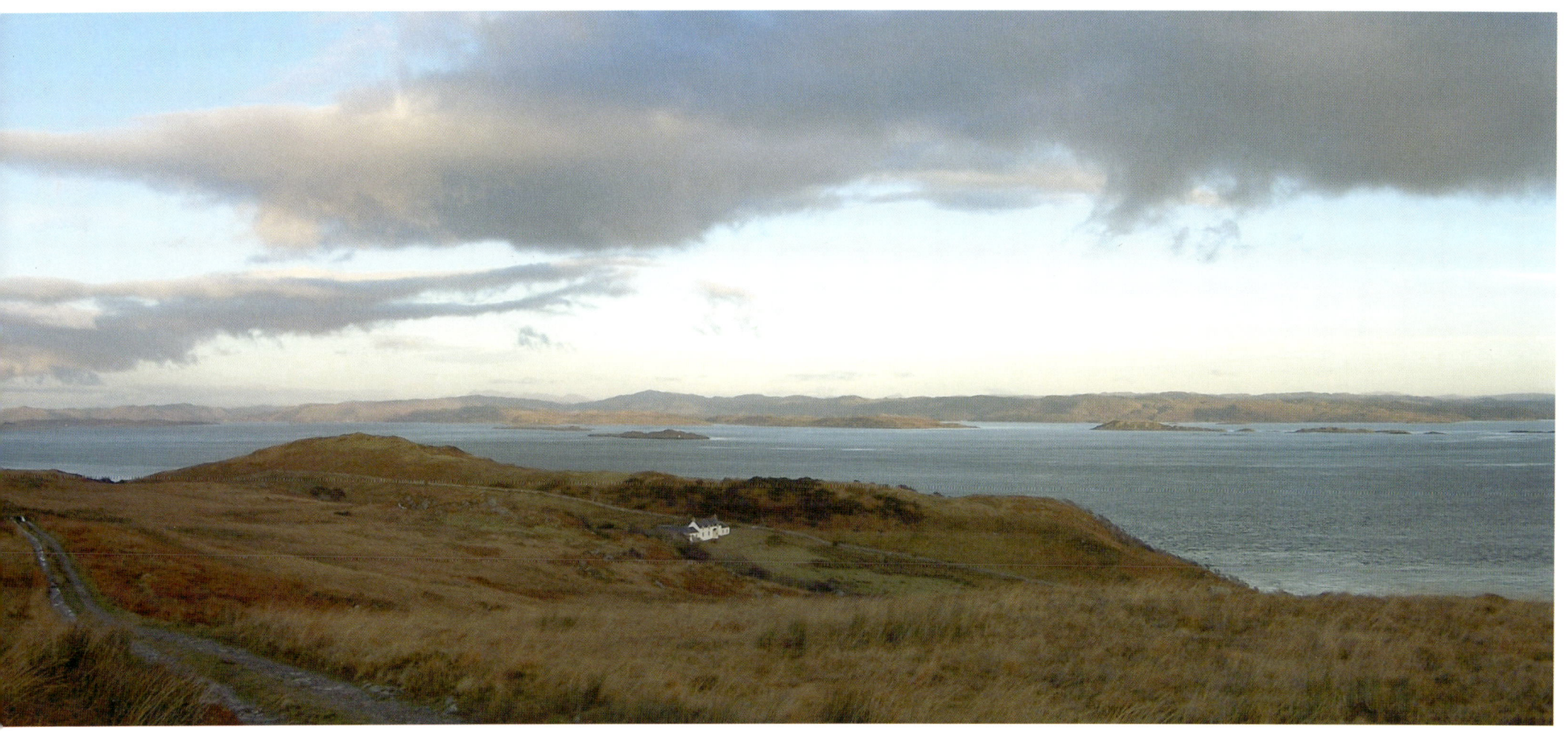

Kinuachdrachd

The headland above the ebb tide

Kinuachdrachd (NR 7050 9870 approx.) is known today as the most remote habitation on the Isle of Jura, with a permanent population of two, excluding geese, a donkey and passing deer. Yet this was once a bustling ferry community complete with a small school house and farms. During the 1930s, much as the inhabitants of St. Kilda had done shortly before them, most of the community left for the Scottish mainland for better homes and the promise of better lives.

Ironically, only a few months after the end of the Second World War the most famous political satirist and novelist of the 20th century came to Kinuachdrachd for a short two week stay, falling in love with the way of life of its two remaining inhabitants and the island itself.. Precisely the kind of people George Orwell had championed early in his literary career – the poor and downtrodden people of the land – were gone from Kinuachdrachd, having abandoned his newly discovered paradise in the Hebrides only a few short years before. Orwell would continue his love affair with Jura at the neighbouring house of Barnhill where he would produce his ultimate and greatest novel, *1984*.

A forever young *Diurach* [native of Jura] remembers George Orwell once bouncing her upon his knee and saying laughingly, "All babies have blue eyes!" This she will never forget.

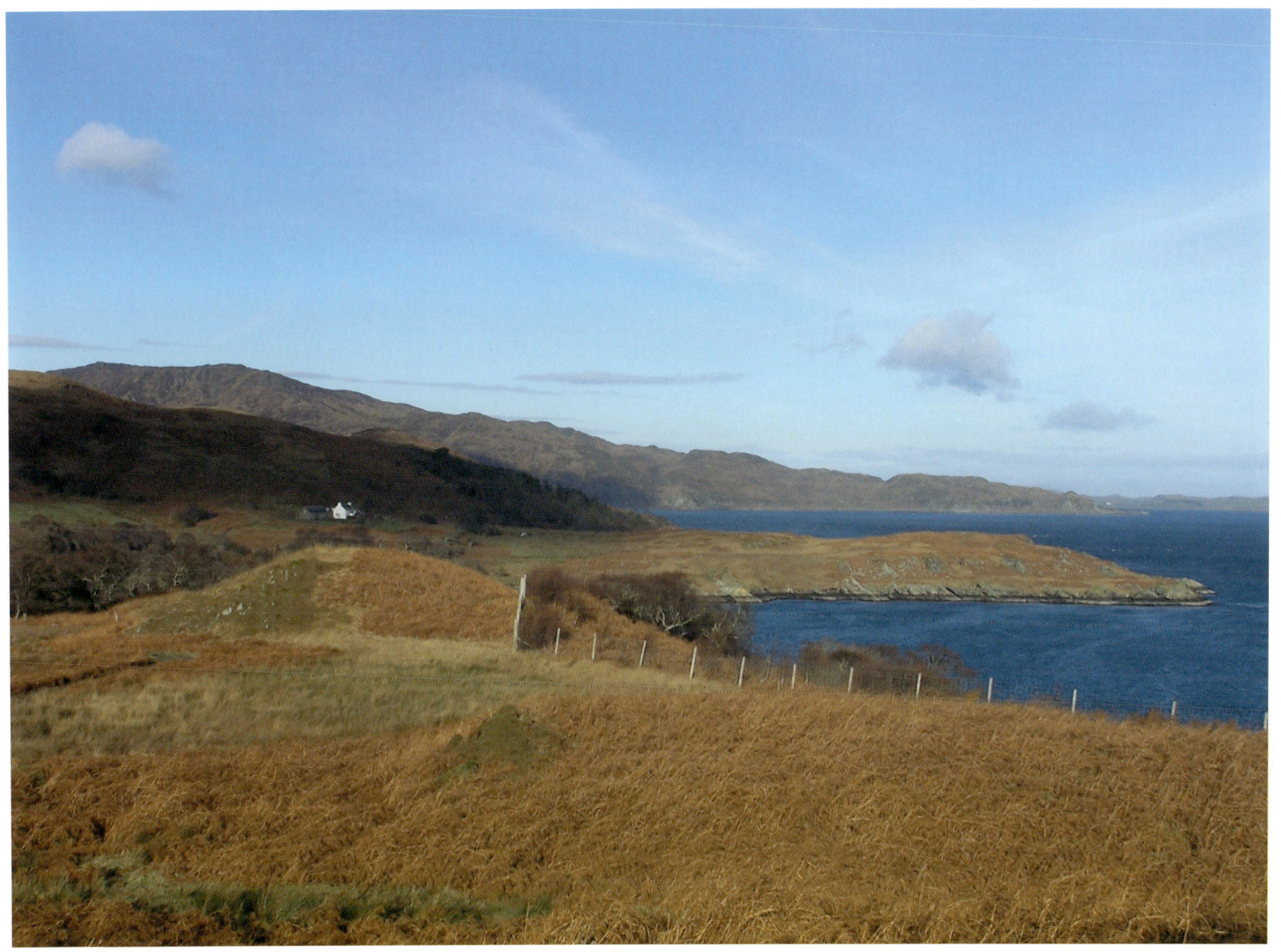

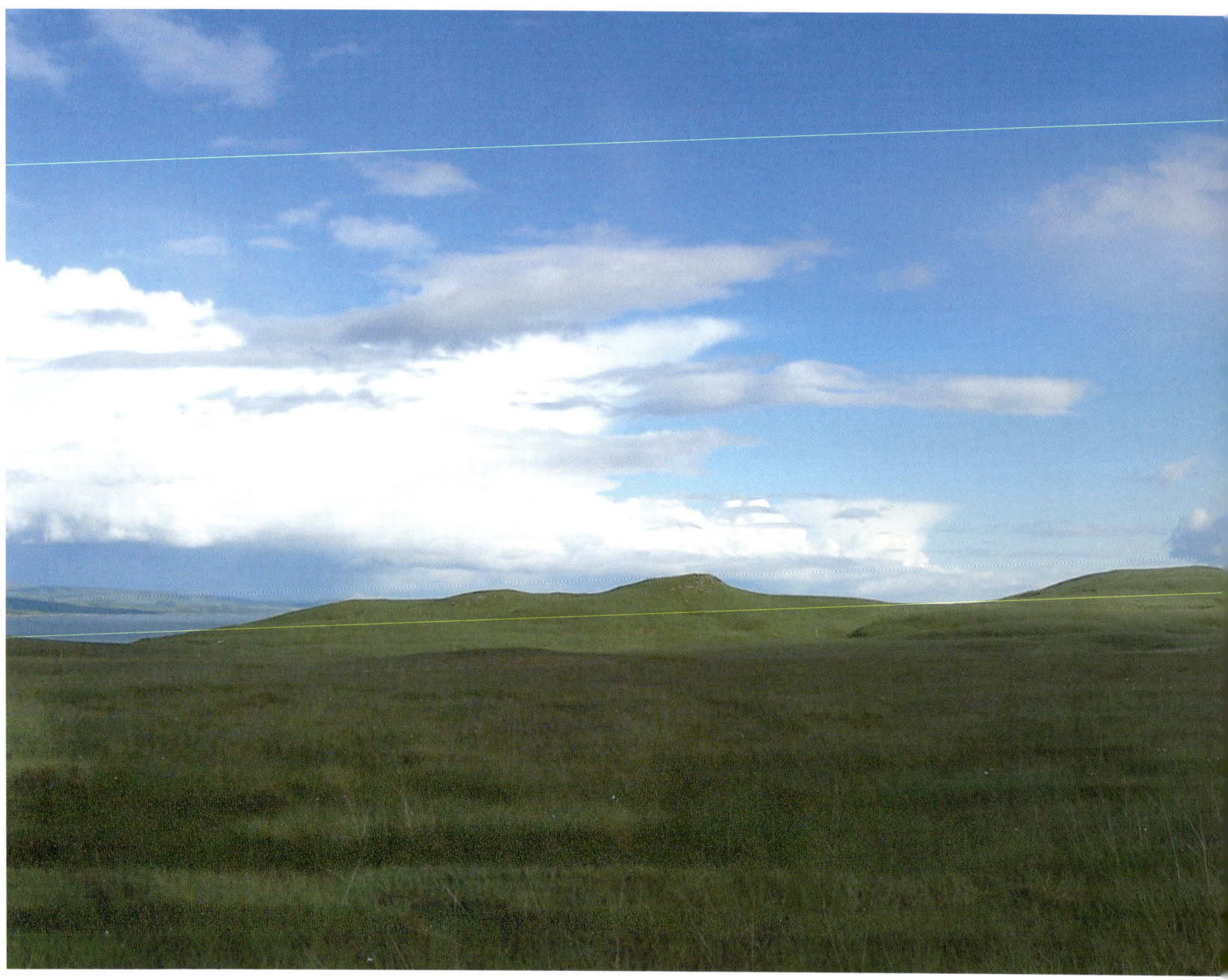

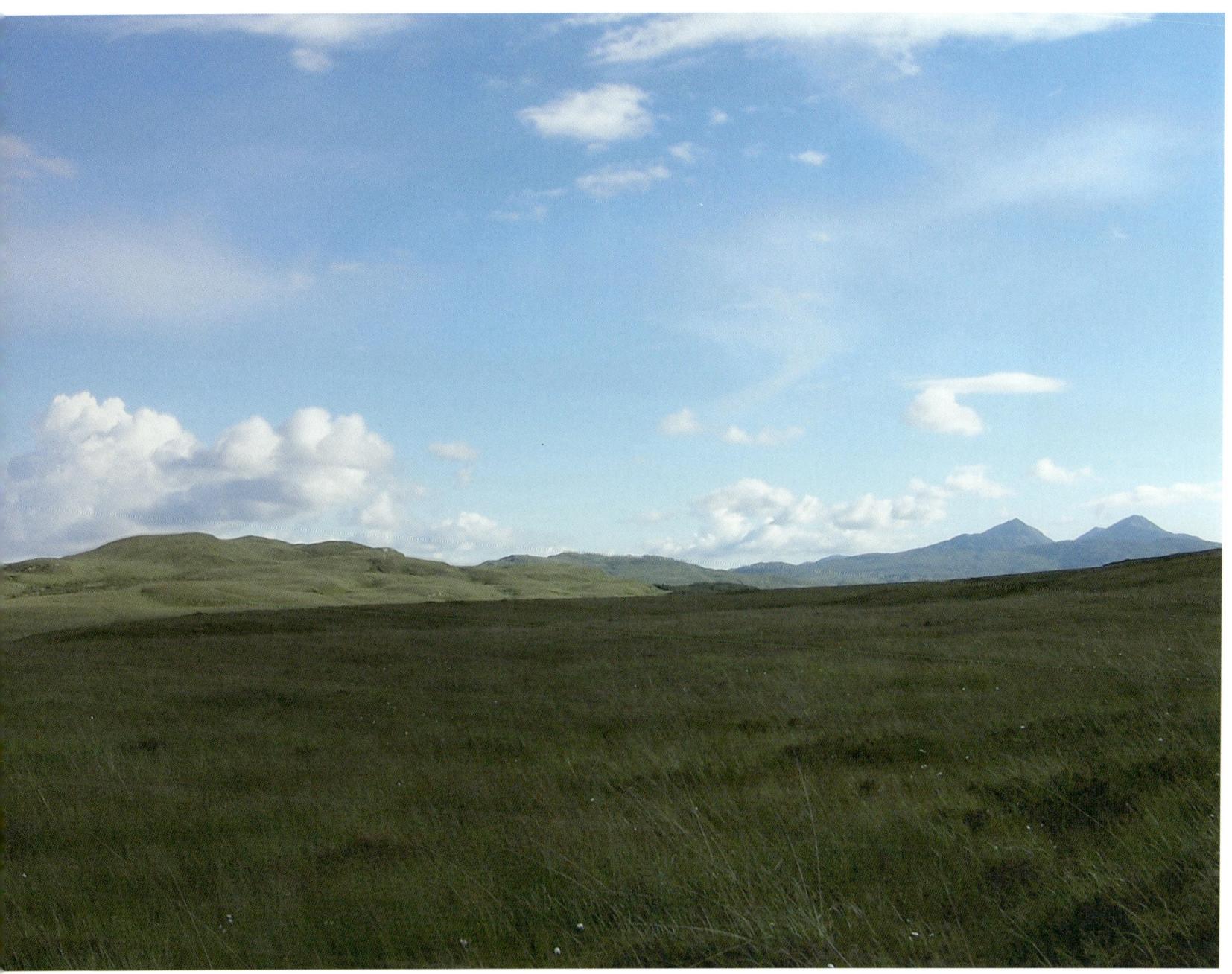

Glengarrisdale

The glen of the triangular-shaped field

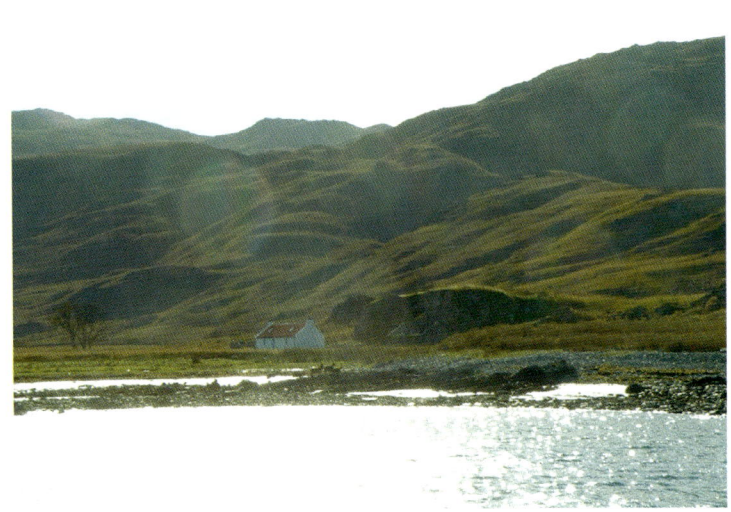

Glengarrisdale (NR 6450 9690 approx.) is today known mostly as the site of a lone bothy offering temporary respite for backpackers and day trippers wishing to visit Jura's remote north-west coast. Yet the small *cnoc* [hill] just above the bothy was once the site of *An Aros* [The Palace], a fortified house belonging to the MacLeans of Duart and, at that time, of Jura as well. A stopping off point for travellers, traders and raiders from both islands and the nearby mainland, Glengarrisdale became a natural battleground. This story recounts one of these conflicts between the MacLeans of Duart and Jura and the Campbells of Craignish and Jura.

A party of MacLeans, who were in possession of Jura at the time, landed on the mainland (Knapdale) to wage war on the Campbells of Craignish, who had apparently gone to north Jura and sacked *An Aros*. The Campbells, having been attacked in their homeland by the MacLeans, vowed to return and increase their sack of north Jura.

The Campbells laid their plans well as this time they landed near Ardlussa, but still they were spotted by a MacLean lookout. The lookout tried to warn his fellow kinsmen around Glengarrisdale, but he was captured and tied to a stake in *Camas nam Meanbh-chuileag* [Bay of the Midge] where he was virtually tortured to death by the bites of the insects. The Campbells, continuing on their way over the hill to Glengarrisdale, found no more lookouts as the MacLeans were practising at their games and without their arms nearby. The Campbells fell upon the MacLeans and wholesale massacre was committed with only one MacLean escaping to spend the night on an island in the Corryvreckan. This MacLean escaped to Duart to raise the great house of MacLean, which soon revisited a great devastation upon the Campbells of Craignish.

Still, the slaughter that the Campbells committed on this day was such that skulls and bones were found with sword cuts and creases for many years afterwards.

The famous "MacLean's Skull" was still to be found in its resting place at a cave near the Glengarrisdale bothy well into the 1970s, when it finally disappeared. Until that time local legend had been that, if the skull were removed, it would return to its resting place by morning. It may be that a loyal MacLean descendant finally gave it a decent burial; even so, it is still one of the island's most enigmatic stories.

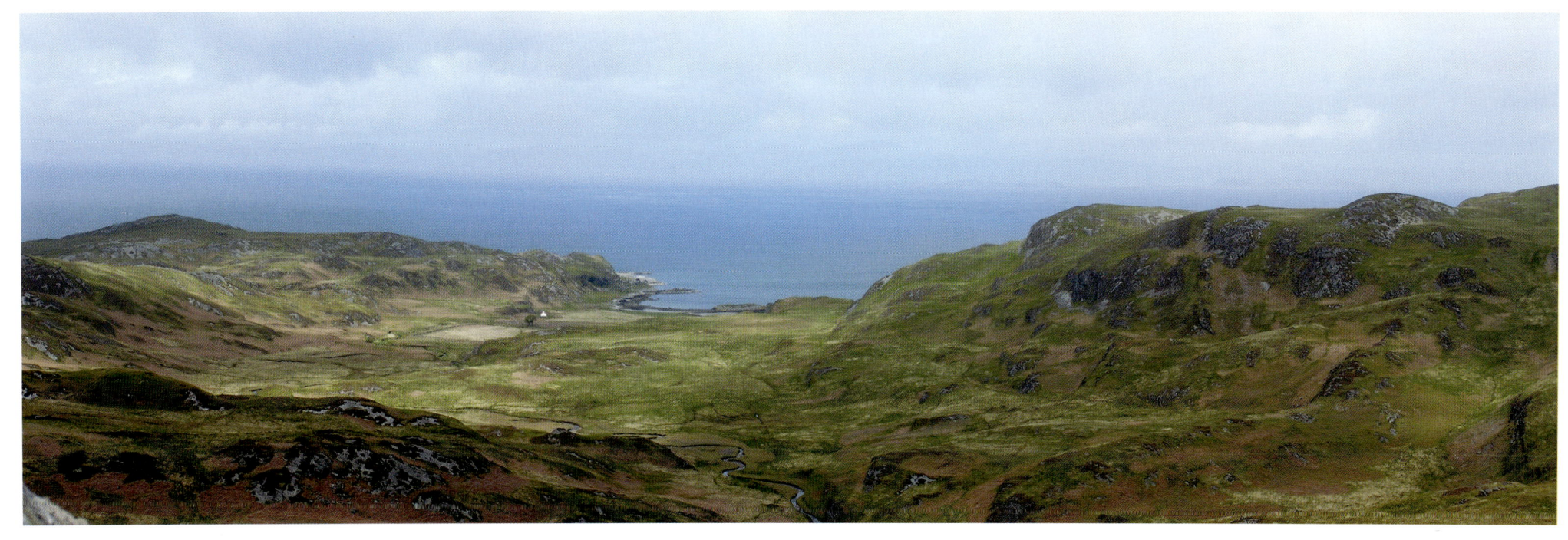

Ardlussa

The high shining or lustrous ground

Ardlussa (NR 6490 8799 approx.) was reckoned by the late Calum MacArthur, an ardent student of Gaelic place names on Jura, to be derived from an earlier Norse word, *ljoss,* meaning glossy, lustrous or shining. In the spring or early summer, when the flowers are in bloom along its wooded coastline and verdant meadows, this interpretation seems more than fitting.

Known as "The Jura Bard", the island's most famous native poet and writer, Donald McKechnie, came from Ardlussa. He wrote this verse, forgotten now by all but a few Gaelic literature specialists. The translator of "An Gleannan" is unknown.

An Gleannan
(from "The Dale", first stanza)

You mild and beautiful glen,
With sylvan slopes as fresh and green.
All creatures love near you to dwell
And listen to the music of your murmuring rill.
Your verdant face with a thousand flowers,
Beneath the balmy air so mild,
The hart and roe in your green bowers,
Bring past scenes again to mind.

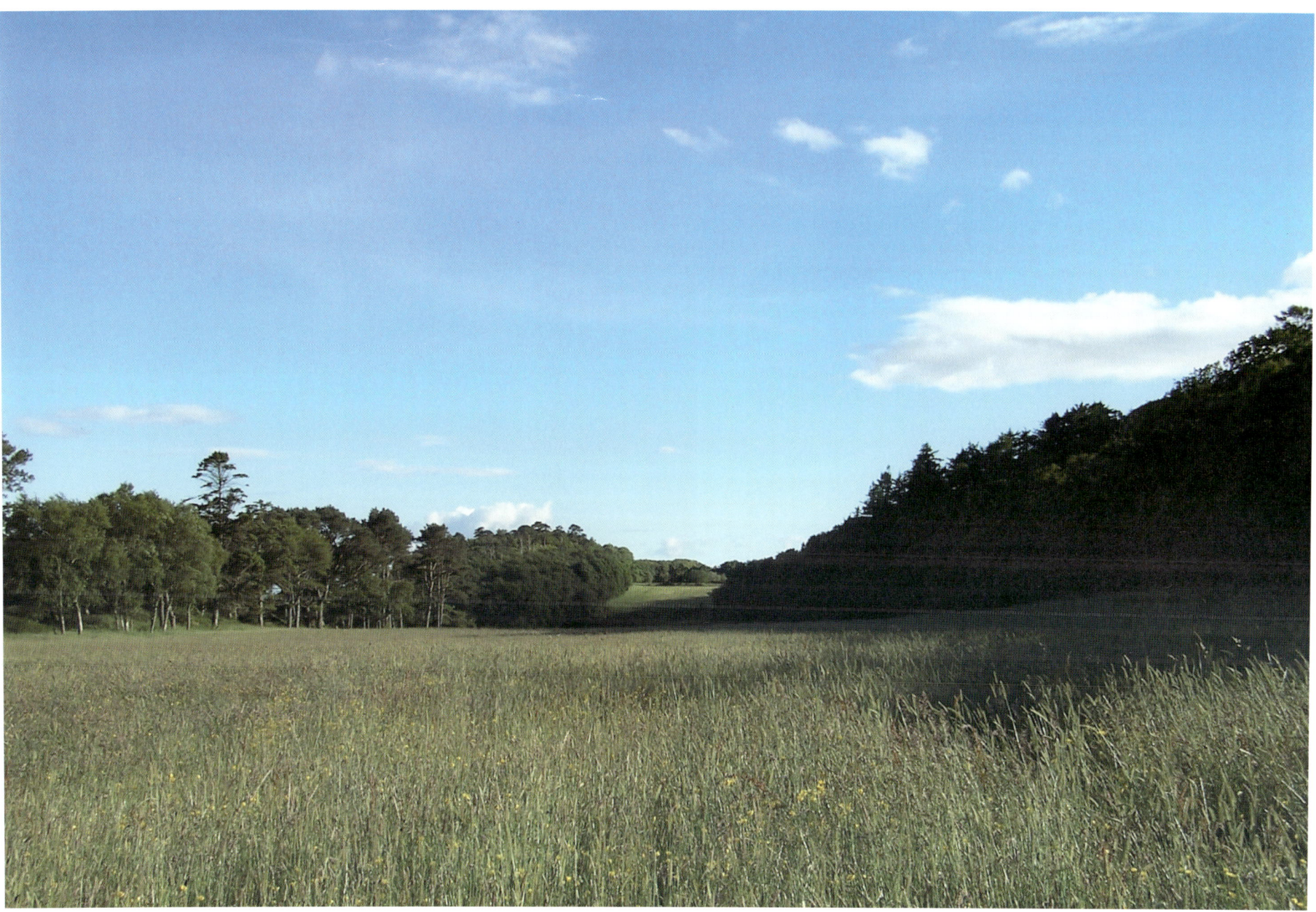

Uamh Dhearg

The Red Cave

Here is a story about Mac 'ille-riabhaich [Darroch] and Am Bàillidh Mór [The Great Steward of Jura] and their stay in Uamh Dhearg (NR 5260 8030 approx.).

Mac 'ille-riabhaich and Am Bàillidh Mór, an ancestor of the Campbells of Jura, were once passing the night together – along with their companions – in Uamh Dhearg, located at the mouth of Glen Batrick.

The cave gets its name from a continual drip of red water falling from its roof. Mac 'lle-riabhaich, having tried to escape the constant dripping by moving about the cave, was enraged when Am Bàillidh Mór commented, "It is no wonder that the red drop will always find you"; this was because Mac 'ille-riabhaich had a fearsome reputation.

Mac 'ille-riabhaich turned to Am Bàillidh Mór and said in a voice as cold as death that, "if it were a blood feud [I] would put the sword to neck if needed be!". Am Bàillidh Mór, upon hearing this, made some excuse to leave the cave and fled, not stopping until he reached the far side of the island.

The Bàillidh Mór referred to in this story may be Dunacha Maol or "Bald Duncan" Campbell, 1st Steward of Jura, son of the Laird of Lochnell and great-grandson of Colin Campbell, 3rd Earl of Argyll. If so, then this story dates from no earlier than 1620 and no later than 1695. There was another branch of Campbells prior to this line who are known to have been stewards as well and if this story refers to the earlier steward, then it would date to around 1506. Thus at the time when Jura fell from the even-handed ownership of the MacDonalds and under the control of the Campbells, a dark period for the island that would last three centuries.

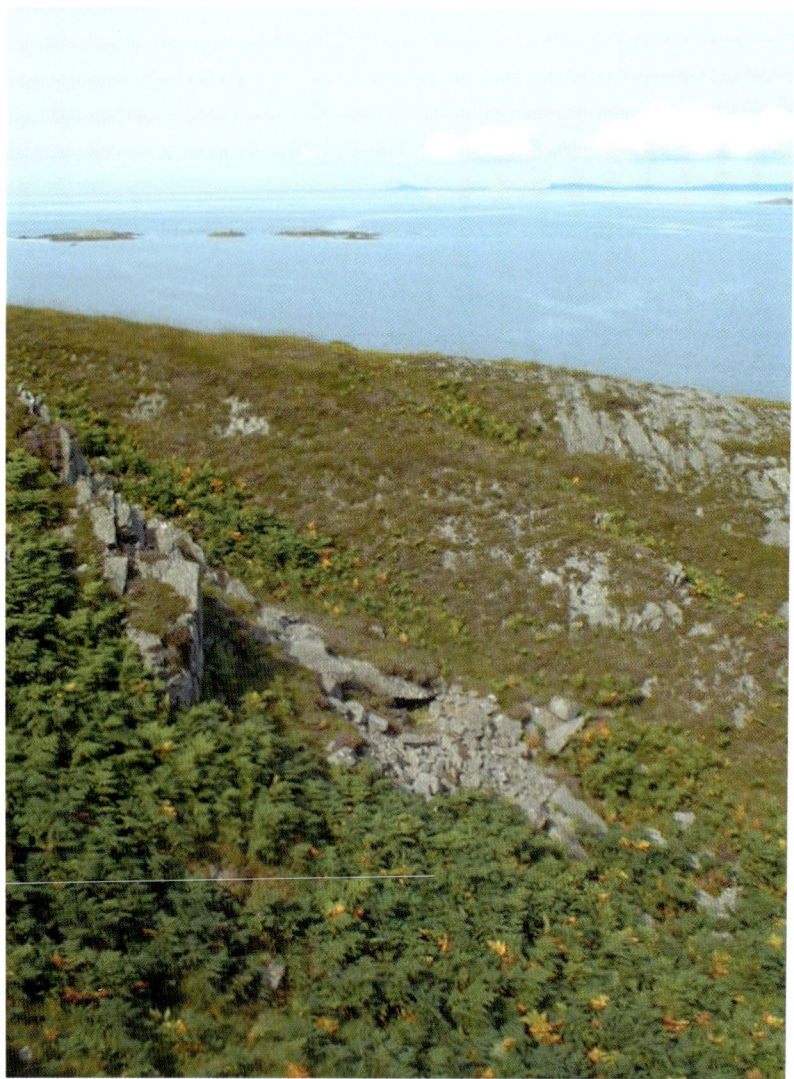

Tarbert

The crossing place of the boat

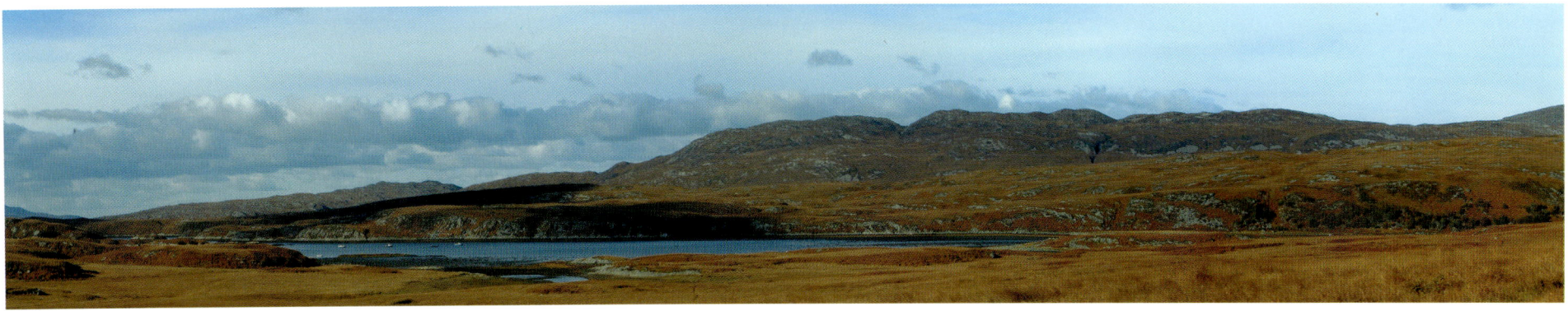

Loch Tarbert nearly bisects the Isle of Jura. Stretching from the west of the island for some 10 kilometres, the great sea loch falls only 900 metres short of dividing the island in two. The mere strip of land that holds the great isle together is known as Tarbert (NR 6130 8210), or "the crossing place of the boat". There may be an allegorical meaning as well; in the following tale, Tarbert was the crossing place between life and death.

There was a married couple at Tarbert whose children were all dying in infancy. A remedy for this was suggested by a *cailleach* [old woman], who said: "Take the skull in Uamh Mhaol an t-Sornaich at Loch Tarbert after sunset. Make gruel in the skull and give it to the afflicted child, but make sure the skull is returned to the *uamh* [cave] before sunrise". The *cailleach* told the parents to do this until the child was cured, always being careful to get the skull from the *uamh* after sunset and to return it before sunrise.

This remedy for an ailment suffered by newly born infants has been documented by historians and observers of the Highlands and Islands of Scotland. One of the earliest reports was by Martin Martin, during his travels through the Hebrides in 1695.

Glenbatrick, seen from Loch Rígh Beag, with the Paps of Jura beyond.

Féith Bhán, one of Jura's famed raised beaches with Loch Tarbert beyond

Cille Challuim-chille and Tobar Challuim-chille

The Church of St. Columba and the Holy Well of St. Columba

Cille Challuim-chille, located at Tarbert Bay (NR 6090 8220 approx.), is known in early Jura history as Kilmhoire, which is more convincing evidence for it having been established in the Columban era, than its current name. Dedicating churches to St. Mary was a common occurrence during the early Celtic Church period (there was also one on the Isle of Scarba) and miracles were commonly associated with them.

Oddly enough, the continuing miracle for those who lived near this ancient ruin was the "lost" *tobar*, or holy well, of Columba. The well is noted on early Ordnance Survey maps, but an early 1980s Royal Commission of the Ancient and Historical Monuments of Scotland survey team was unable to locate it, and pronounced it lost. However, numerous *Diurachs* [natives of Jura] know its whereabouts and this author located it easily in 2003. Local oral legend notes that even in drought years the holy well of Columba never ran dry, surely also a miracle. There is also a "lost" holy man's cave nearby, adding another layer of intrigue.

W.J. Watson, the eminent Celtic historian of the 20th century, argued that Jura was St. Columba's Hinba. With this in mind, here is a short passage from Adomnan's "Life of St. Columba" (trans. Richard Sharpe):

Once, four saints who had founded monasteries in Ireland came to visit St. Columba. When they arrived at Hinba they found him there. The names of these famous men were St. Cainnech, St. Brendan, St. Comgall, and St. Cormac. When the sacred mysteries of the Eucharist were to take place, with one accord they chose St. Columba to be the celebrant…There while the sacred mass was celebrated St. Brendan saw a radiant ball of fire shining very brightly from St. Columba's head as he stood in front of the altar and consecrated the sacred oblation. It shone upwards like a column of light and lasted until the mysteries were completed. Afterwards St. Brendan disclosed what he had seen to St. Comgall and St. Cainnech.

St. Brendan is known in history as St. Brendan the Navigator, and may have sailed to Iceland, Greenland and possibly even America. His voyages were recreated by Tim Severin in the 1970s aboard a sea-going *currach* [skin boat].

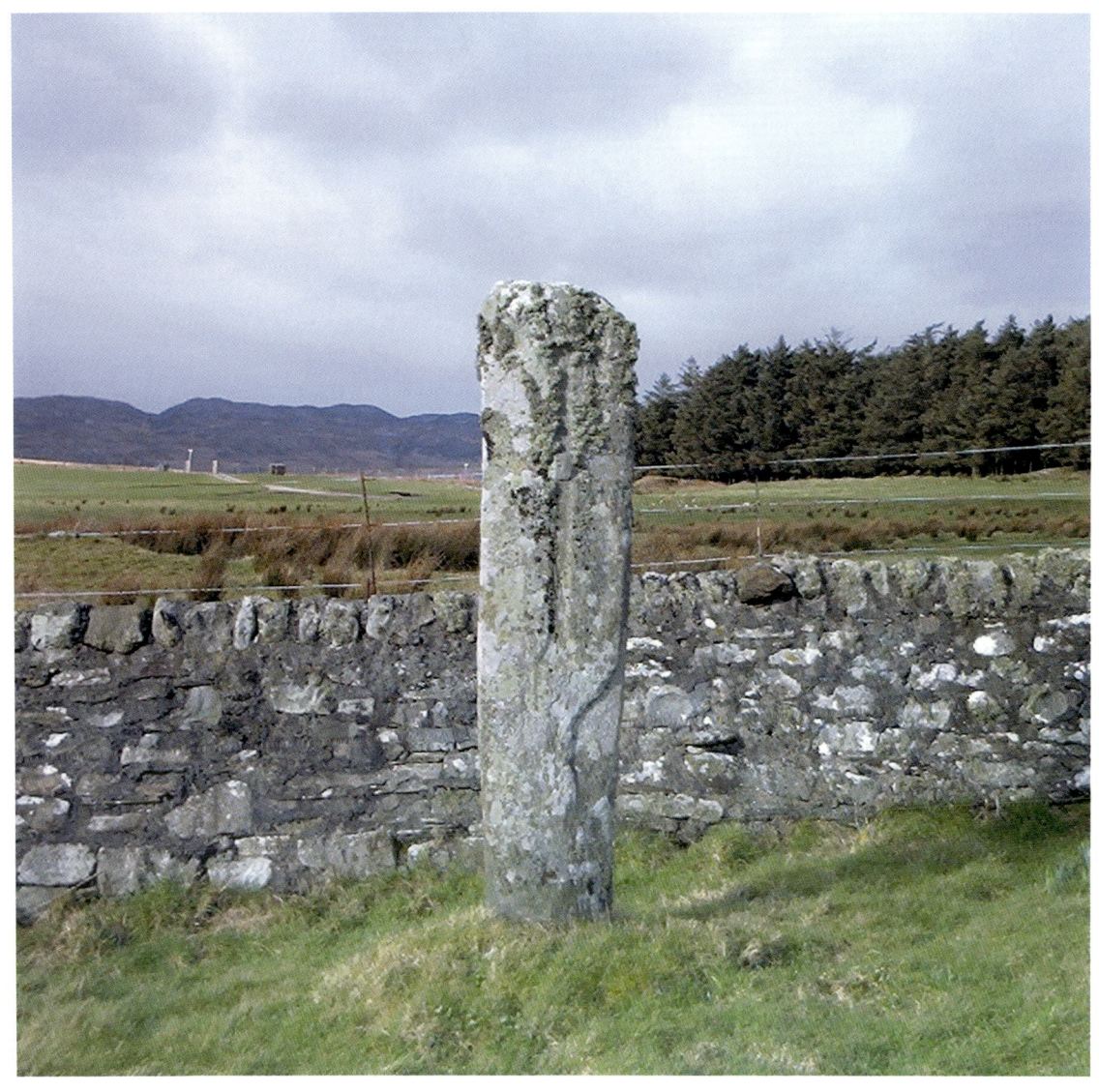

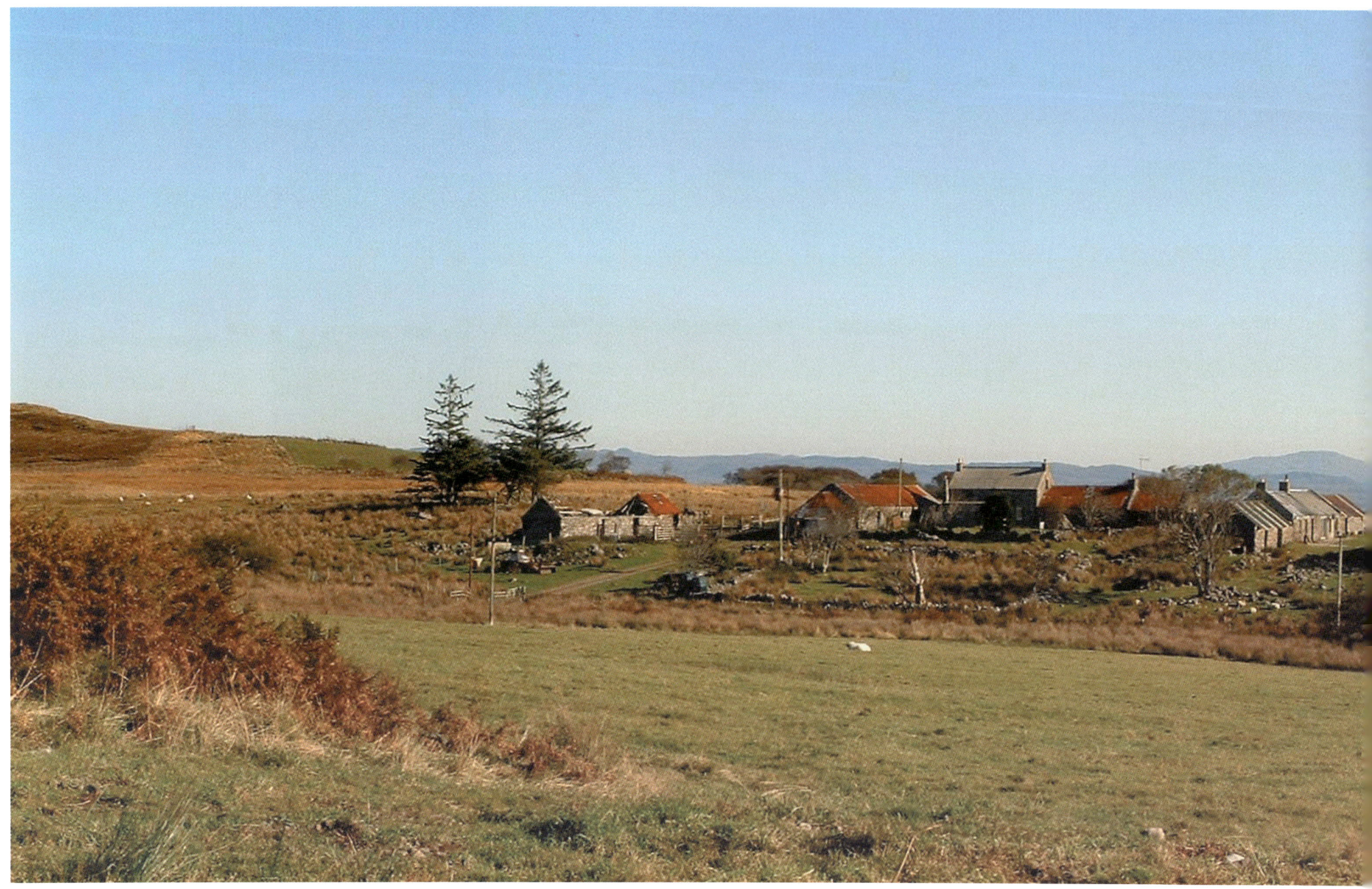

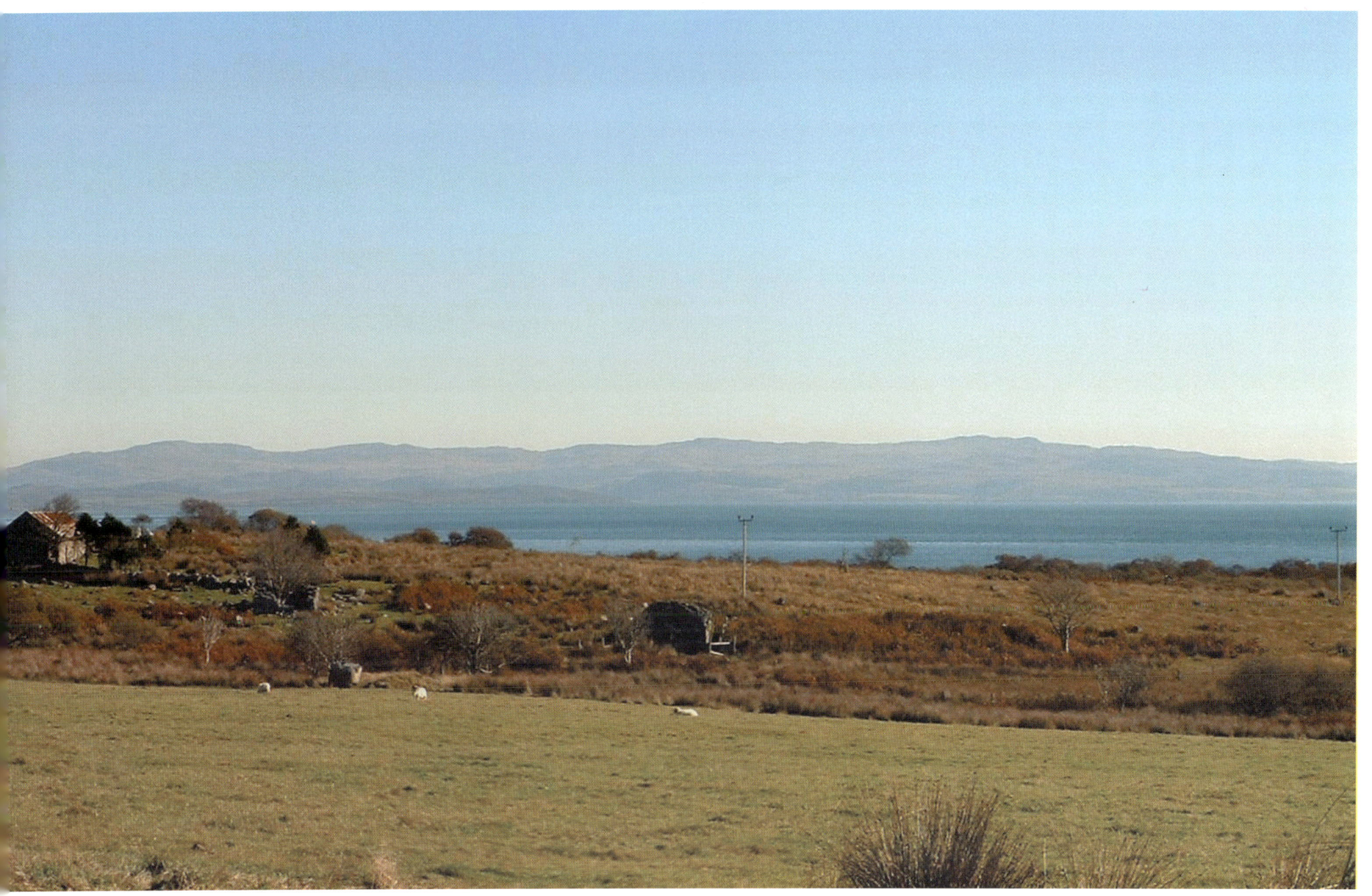

Lowlandman's Bay

Bàgh na Gall

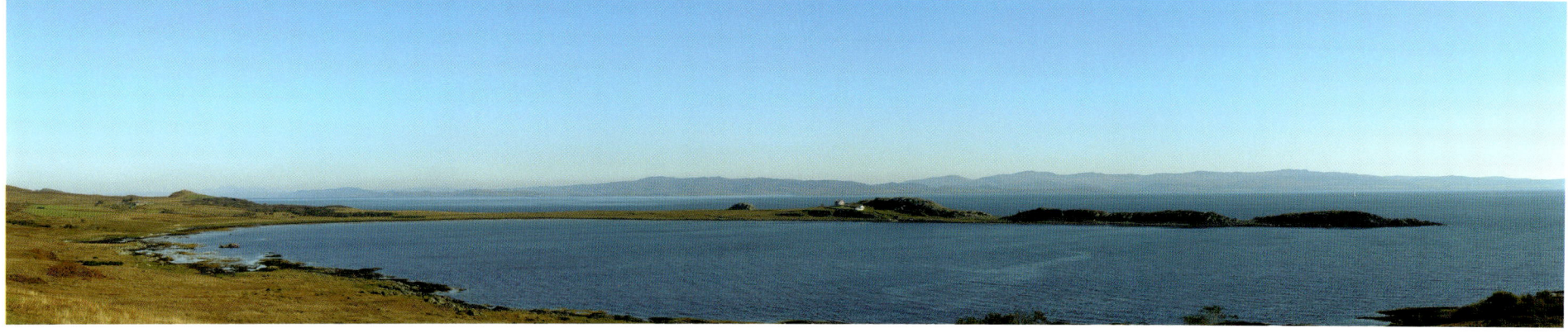

Lowlandman's Bay (NR 5650 7250 approx.) is probably Jura's most perfectly shaped bay with its deep pocketed cove and slender rocky peninsula on its eastern side. In Jura's oral history the bay has always been attributed to mainland traders from the south-west of Scotland (i.e. the Lowlands), who landed there to set up temporary trading posts. This may be supported by the nearby Gaelic place name of A' Mhalairt [The Merchant or Barterer]. The following story concerns the bay's peninsula, Rubh' an Leim [Point of the Leap].

Mhic-Libhir [McLever] was a robber who hid his treasure at the summit of Cnoc na h-Iolaire [Hill of the Eagle] above Loch na Mile (the northern portion of Small Isles Bay: author's note). Mhic-Libhir had been particularly bold in his crimes so a careful watch was laid about to spy him out. Mhic-Libhir was seen against the skyline while atop the *cnoc* [hill] and the alarm was raised. Mhic-Libhir, seeing he was being pursued, raced down from the *cnoc* along the path that ran out along the north side of Lowlandman's Bay. His pursuers were close upon him when the thief decided to chance his luck by leaping the great crevice that splits Rubh' an Leim in two. Managing to gain the other side of the *rubha* [point] – and leaving his pursuers stunned by his mighty leap – Mhic-Libhir then dived into the waters of Lowlandman's Bay. Striking out across the mouth of the bay, Mhic-Libhir reached the shore beneath Ardfarnal Hill and raced across the narrow bit of land until he reached Loch na Mile, where he again dived into the water. Not ceasing for fear of his pursuers, Mhic-Libhir swam until he reached the shore beneath Jura Forest, where he crawled ashore exhausted and crept through the undergrowth into a cave that he knew. Thinking he was safe, the thief fell asleep. However, the pursuing party searched relentlessly through the day and night and almost gave up when loud snoring was heard. Searching quietly through the brush, the search party found Mhic-Libhir sleeping soundly, whereupon he was slain.

Is this story true? Today's Ordnance Survey map carries the Gaelic place names Carraig Mhic 'ill Libhir [the Rock of McLever] and Abhainn Mhic 'ill Libhir [the River of McLever]. Old OS maps carry the place name Uamh na Mhic 'ill Libhir, or "McLever's Cave". Certainly some great event that captured the imagination of the Jura community forever tied the name Mhic 'ill Libhir to this landscape.

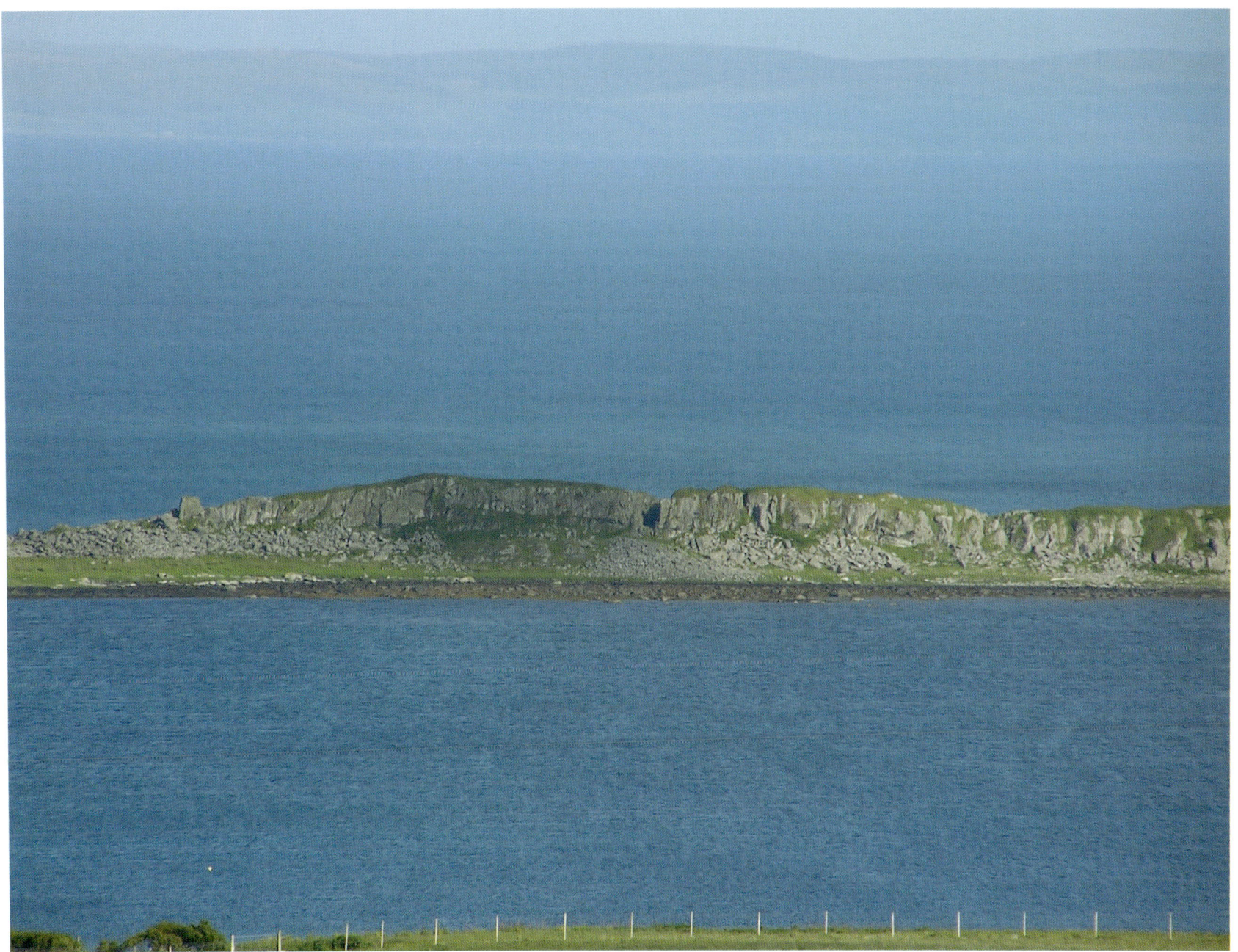

Knockrome-Ardfarnal

The crooked hill and the hill of the priest

Perhaps the earliest known story about today's crofting community of Knockrome-Ardfarnal (NR 5550 7150 approx.) concerns the exploits of "Colkitto", most likely the father of the more well-known Colkitto, commander of the Duke of Montrose's Highland troops during the Covenanters' period. Here, one of the most detailed and entertaining stories of early "historical" Jura is told with wit and humour.

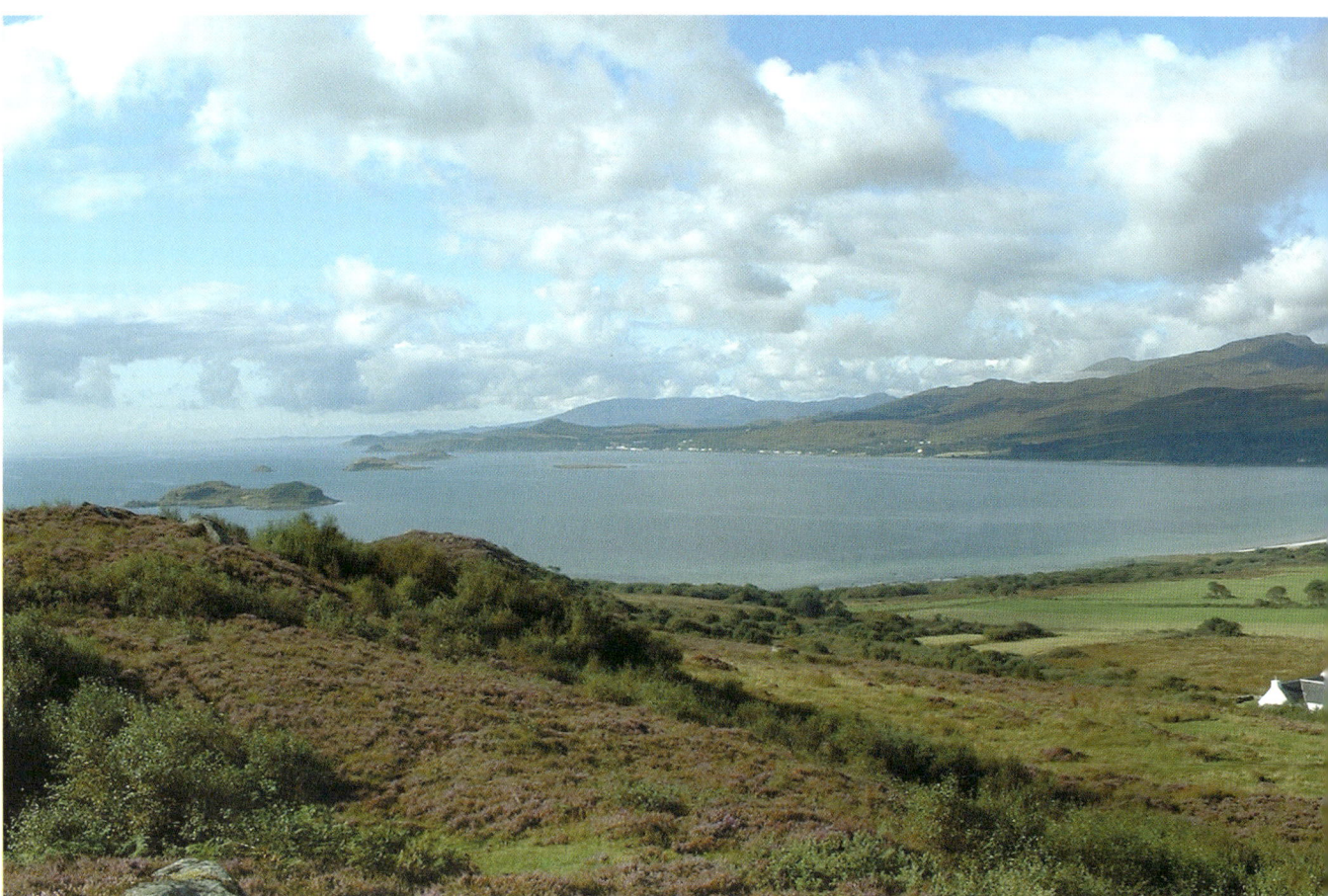

The warrior known as Colkitto was on Jura on one occasion with a number of his followers and was travelling from the south-west of the island up into the west. The son of Fear Craignish [the Laird or Master of Craignish] was also on Jura at the time with other sons and followers of the headmen of Craignish. At nightfall Colkitto intended to encamp at Inverneil and he and his men erected huts for shelter; they also lit a fire and began to prepare a meal. Colkitto, while walking near the camp, saw that another party had also built huts, and on approaching the sentry he asked who was camped there.

The sentry replied that they belonged to the son of Fear Craignish and his followers. Colkitto replied, "I had intended to pass the night here, but since they are here, we shall move on to another place", and he left the watchman. Colkitto's dog, however, went near the tent of young Craignish and Craignish's dog rushed out and fought with Colkitto's dog. Colkitto turned back and, striking Craignish's dog, stopped the fight and walked away with his own dog.

Young Craignish, standing at a distance, asked the watchman, 'Who was that man who passed?' The watchman replied, "That was Colkitto who has a party of men with him". Young Craignish was angry and nothing would satisfy him but to pursue Colkitto. The other sons of the headmen of Craignish tried to dissuade him from following Colkitto but young Craignish would not listen.

Craignish set off with his followers and overtook Colkitto and his men at Knockrome, which is near the sea. He made an attack on Colkitto who at the time was somewhat advanced in years. Craignish, however, was at the fullness of his strength and so it looked as if Colkitto would be slain. The Jura dwarf, known as Dubhshith Macillesheathanach [McDuffie Shaw] was nearby and was armed with a weapon called the *stapull crom* [war club].

Colkitto called out to Dubhsith, 'Have you ever

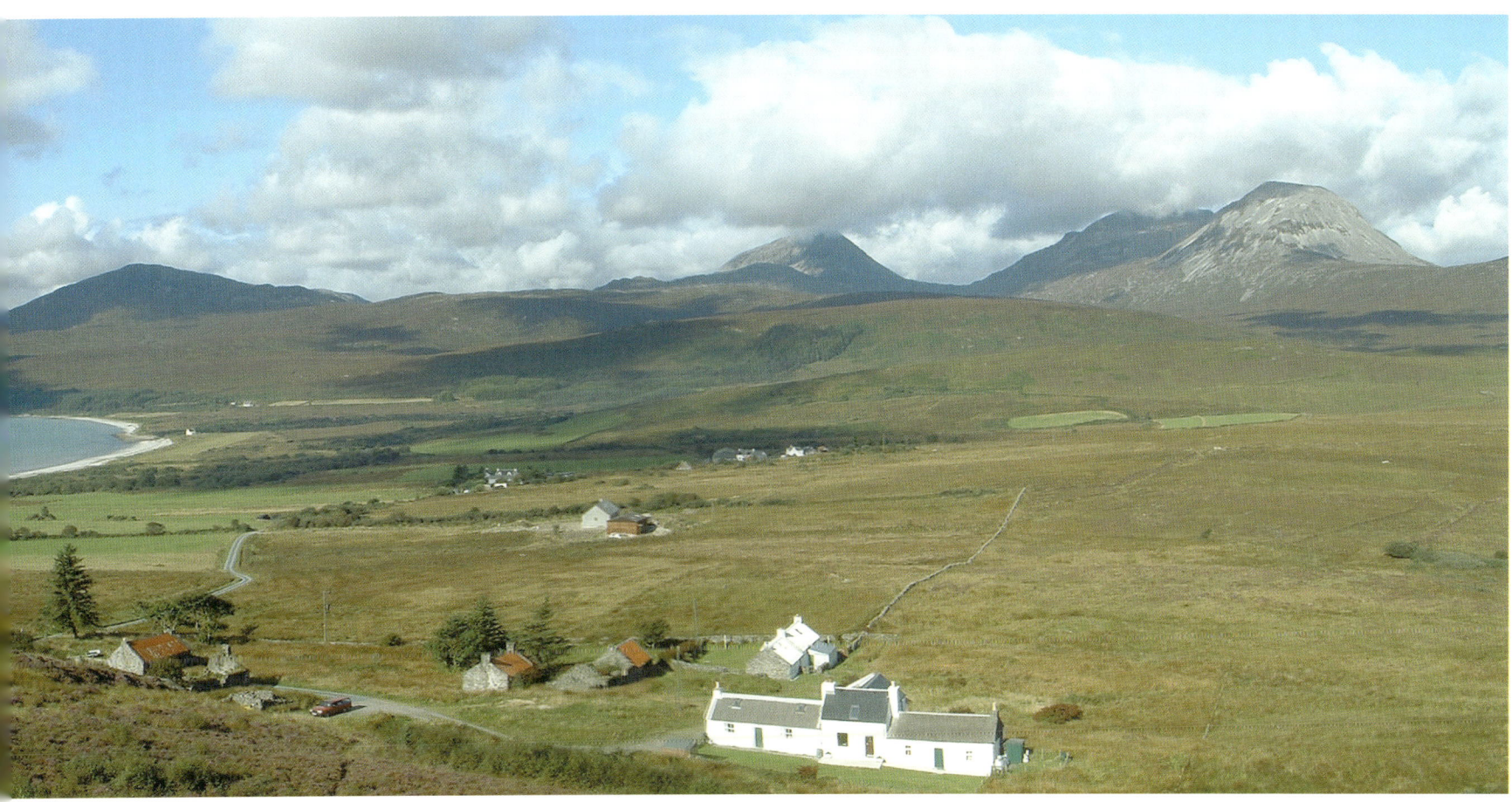

haughed a cow?' Dubhsith swung his weapon out past Colkitto and, aiming a blow at young Craignish, haughed him, whereupon Colkitto killed him outright. (Haughing was a technique where the war club was used to hamstring an opponent, who was then usually dispatched with a sword attack.) Dubhsith followed Colkitto, keeping close to him, and whenever any foe came near him, haughed them, allowing Colkitto to kill them. This would not be the last time that Dubhsith would figure large in a Jura legend.

Thus, young Craignish and forty of his men were killed in the fight that took place at Knockrome, while Colkitto escaped injury. The end result was that an older, wiser man who could control his dog destroyed a proud young man who could not control his own dog.

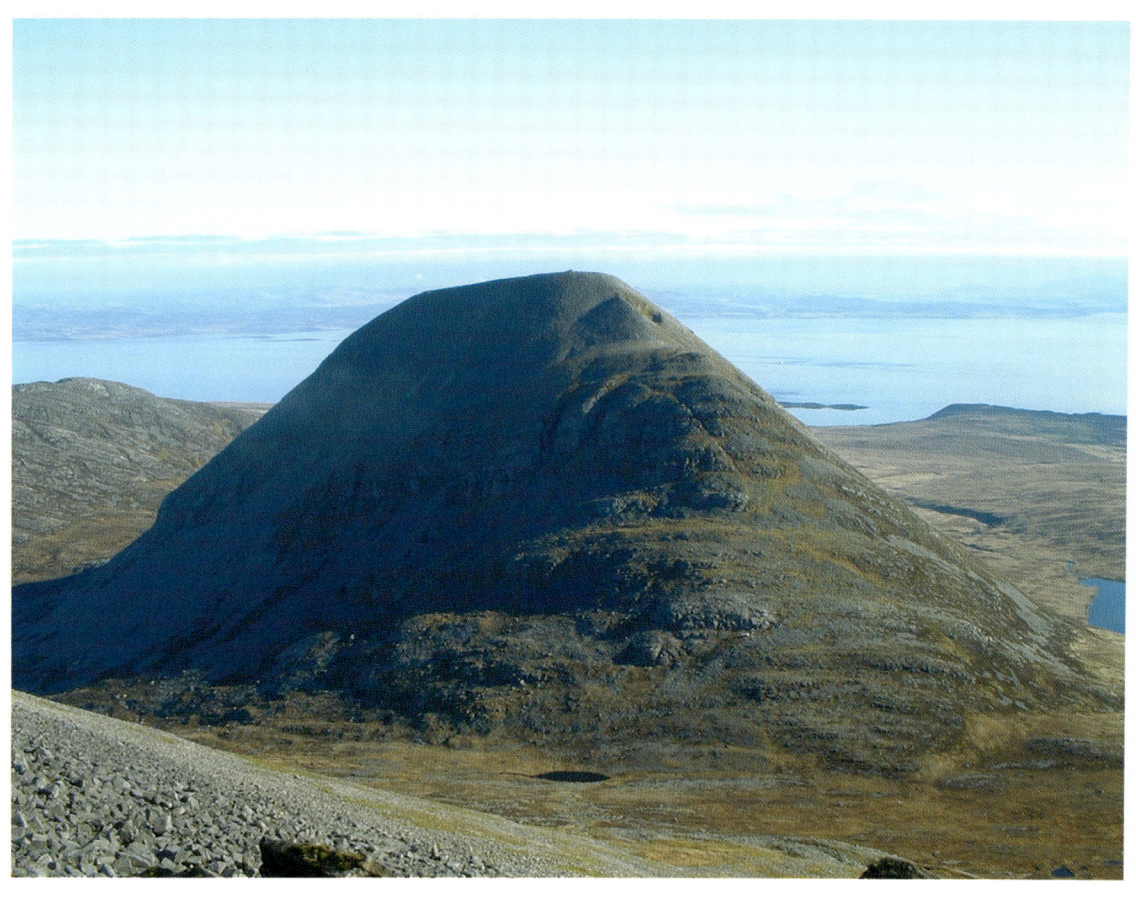

Leargybreck

The dappled sloping hill

Leargybreck (NR 5380 7120 approx.) is marked today by only two forlorn structures, an abandoned church and a former home, both now converted into holiday cottages. In the distant past Leargybreck was widely known as the home of the Mhic 'ille-bhuidhe, or the Buies of Leargybreck as they were called. While the Gaelic word *bhuidhe* is commonly translated today into English as "yellow", it is likely that "golden" is the more correct interpretation. This may seem a minor detail, but when one considers that the Buies are usually mentioned as close relatives of the MacDonalds, or Lords of the Isles, their surname becomes an important clue.

It is known that Somerled, the original ancestor of all the MacDonald clans, was himself a product of Norse and Irish ancestry – as was much of the area bordering the Irish Sea around 1100 AD. The predominant political and military power throughout the west of Scotland from approximately 700 AD until the rise of Somerled in 1156 AD was Norwegian. It stands to reason that, after four and a half centuries, more than a few marriages had taken place in the region and that the gene that causes fair hair would have been spread far and wide. The Buies themselves surely travelled far and wide, as is evidenced by their ancestral burial ground at Cill Earnadail, where five extraordinary grave slabs give mute testimony to their prowess, wealth and faith. Dated between the 12th and 14th centuries, these crumbling markers can be distinguished by the long swords carved into their surfaces and have been interpreted by some as the symbols of "crusader knights". This may be fanciful thinking, but it is well known that during the 13th and 14th centuries many Scottish men of arms did venture afar to places like Spain to fight the "enemies of God". It may be then that the Buies resting at Cill Earnadail were just such men and, if so, it is a testimony to their faith that they desired to be buried near the presumed grave of St. Ernán, rather than only a short distance away at their ancestral home on the dappled sloping hill of Leargybreck.

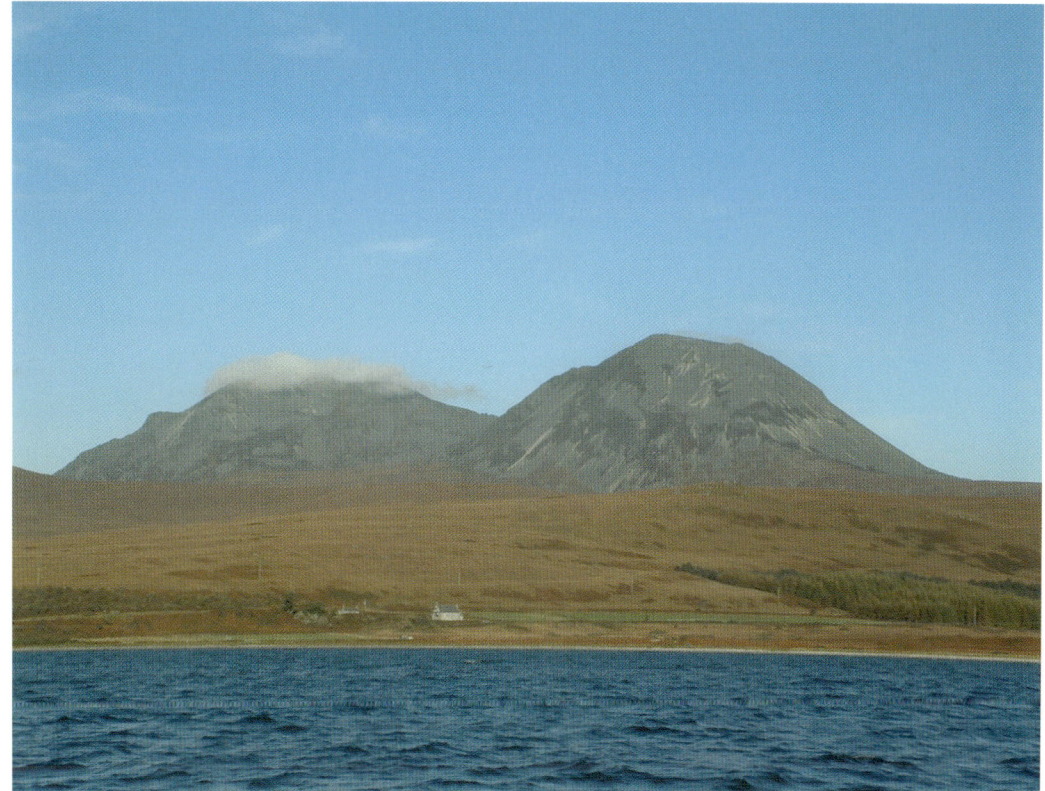

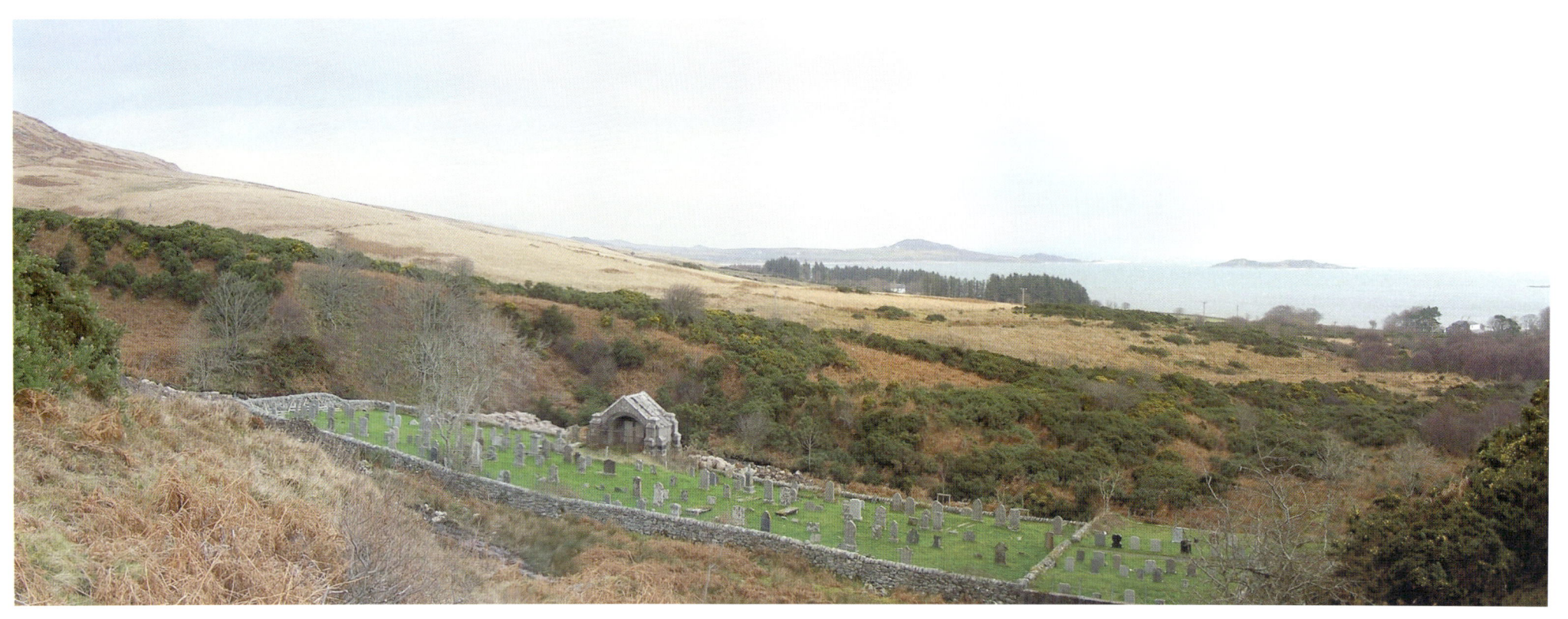

Cille Earnadail [the Church of St. Ernán] and the Forgotten Saint

Many oral legends in the Highlands and Islands of Scotland have become so distorted with time, and the gentle wear of weakening memories, that they have become wholly unrecognisable from their original intent. However, on the Isle of Jura there is one legendary story that is so strongly tied to an identifiable place and the earliest written document of the Hebrides that it becomes imbued with a certain sense of truth. This is the story of St. Ernán, Scotland's greatest forgotten saint and the uncle of St. Columba, who himself was Scotland's original patron saint.

The Saint's prophecy about the priest Ernán (from Adomnan's *Life of St. Columba* translated by Richard Sharpe)

Likewise once the reverend man (i.e. St. Columba – author's note) sent his elderly uncle, Ernán, a priest, to be prior of the monastery he had founded years before on the Island of Hinba. When he was ready to set out, St. Columba kissed him and blessed him, speaking these prophetic words:

"I do not hope to see again in this earthly life this friend of mine now setting out on his journey."

Not many days had passed before Ernán was taken ill, and by his own wish was taken back to Iona to St. Columba. When told of his arrival, the saint was glad and set out to the harbour to meet him. Ernán, though he was a sick man, made every effort to try to go to the saint on his feet. But when there was less than fifty yards between them, death suddenly caught up with Ernán. He fell to the ground and breathed his last before the saint could set eyes on his face alive. Otherwise the saint's word would have proved false.

In the place where Ernán died, in front of the door of the corn-kiln, a cross was set up, and another on the spot where St. Columba was standing at the moment of St. Ernán's death. These are still standing today.

The Isle of Hinba mentioned in the above story has been argued to be the Isle of Jura by several scholars through the years, including W.J. Watson, who's titanic *History of the Celtic Place-Names of Scotland* is highly regarded even today. Hinba was the island that St. Columba used as his spiritual retreat and where he had his famous struggle with an angel of God. Yet, it is this marvellous legend of St. Ernán's burial that may provide the strongest support for Jura's claim to be St. Columba's "blessed isle".

So, we continue the story by recounting Jura's most beautiful legend which tells the story of the burial of St. Ernán:

The aged saint died while away from Jura, but before dying gave instruction concerning his burial. His body was to be transported back to Jura and carried onward until the burial party came upon a small glen that had a mist hanging over it. They were to stop and bury his body in that spot. The burial party followed his instructions and landed upon the south-west shores of Jura at a rock known as Leac Ernán, and continued across the island until they came to the place described by the saint. There in the small glen with a mist above it the followers of St. Ernán laid the uncle of St. Columba to rest. The place where the saint was buried is now the churchyard of Cille Earnadail (Kilearnadil).

While Cille Earnadail or Kilearnadil ceased to be the parish church for Jura many centuries ago, it is the only church in Scotland known to be dedicated to St. Ernán and to be approximately contemporary with his actual existence. Furthermore, the place names of *Leac Ernan* and *Cille Earnadail* are still in existence today on current Ordnance Survey maps along with one other place name usually overlooked, *Ath nam Marbh*. Translated from the Gaelic as the "ford of the dead", the *ath* lies along the ancient route from the south-west of Jura to Cille Earnadail.

However, St. Ernán's most important legacy to the world was left long before he came to the Hebrides. Once, while studying with his teacher, Gemmán, St. Columba saw a young woman brutally murdered in front of them, even after attempting to intervene and save her life. St. Columba pronounced a sentence upon the woman's killer that he would die when the woman's soul ascended to heaven. It is said that afterwards St. Columba told his uncle, St. Ernán, and his mother, St. Eithne, about the event, upon which they told the saint that there should be a law protecting women, children and places of worship. It was St. Columba's biographer, St. Adomnán, who would create the religious pronouncement known to history as "The Law of Innocents".

St. Ernán, then, should be remembered as one of the creators of the first laws concerning "crimes against humanity". Instead he is forgotten in an increasingly secular world, except by the people of Jura, who faithfully remember his devotion.

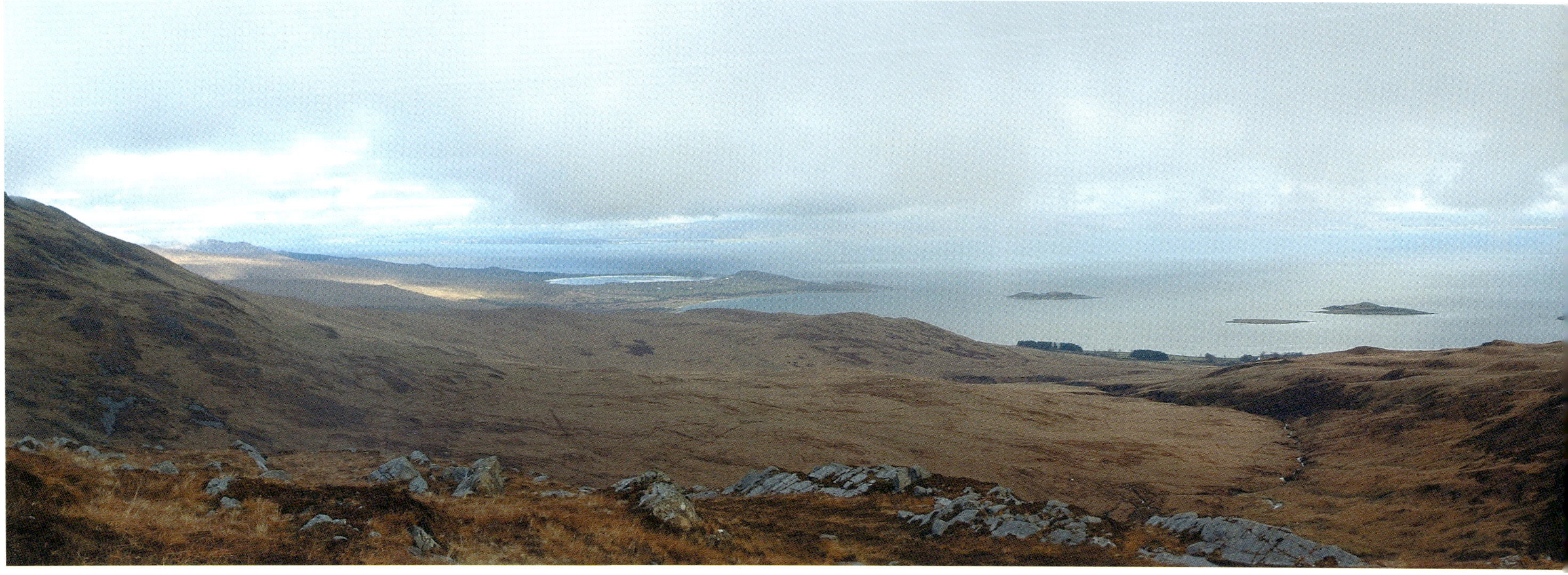

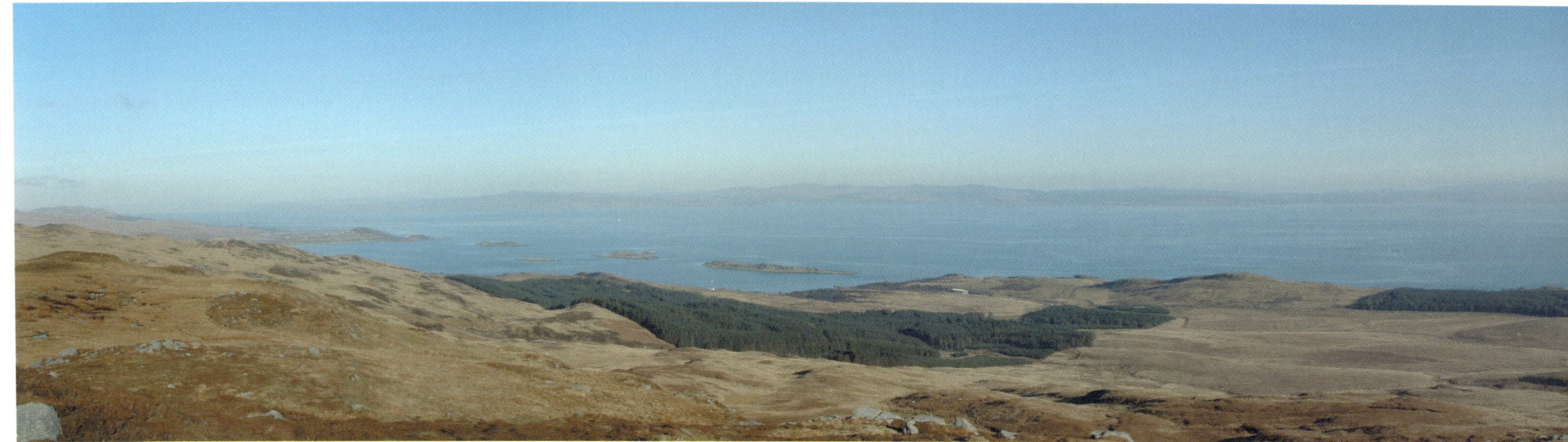

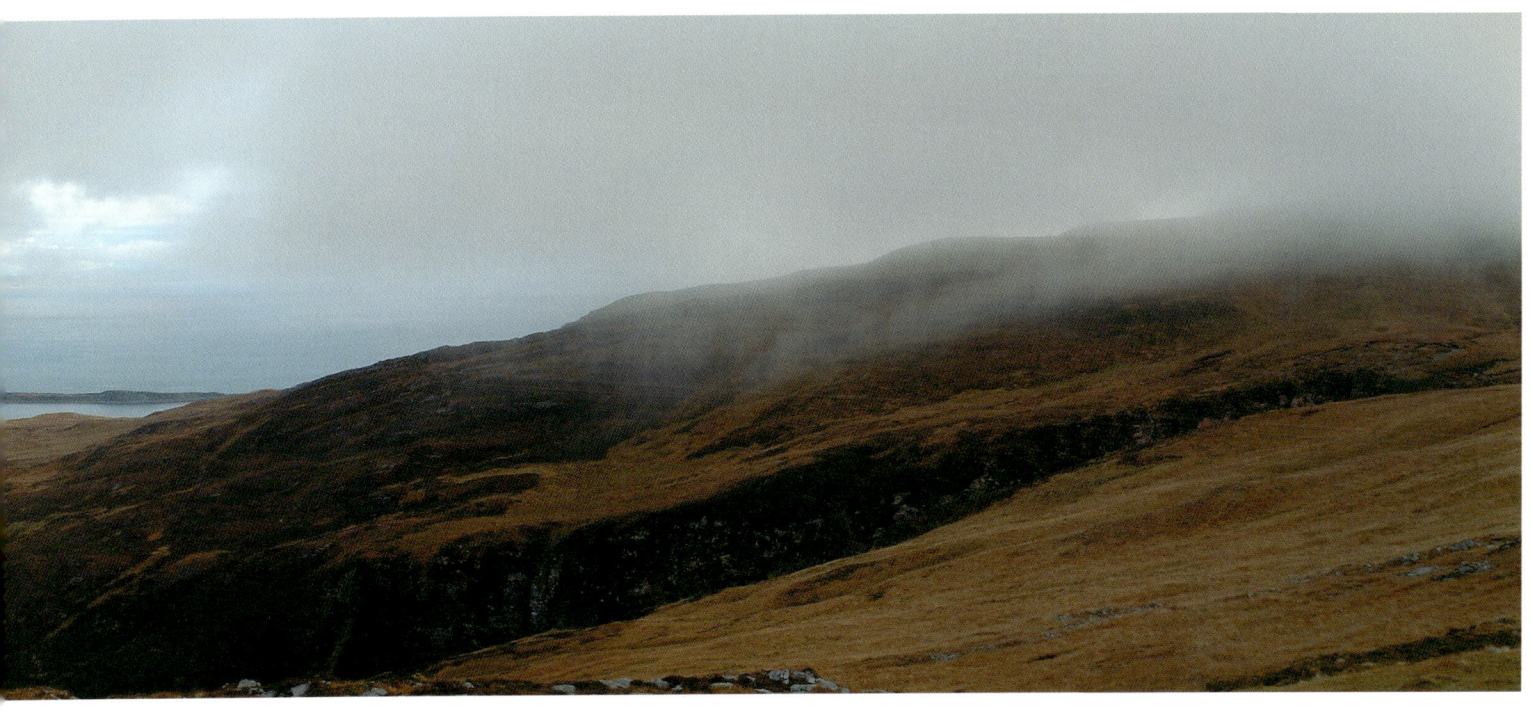

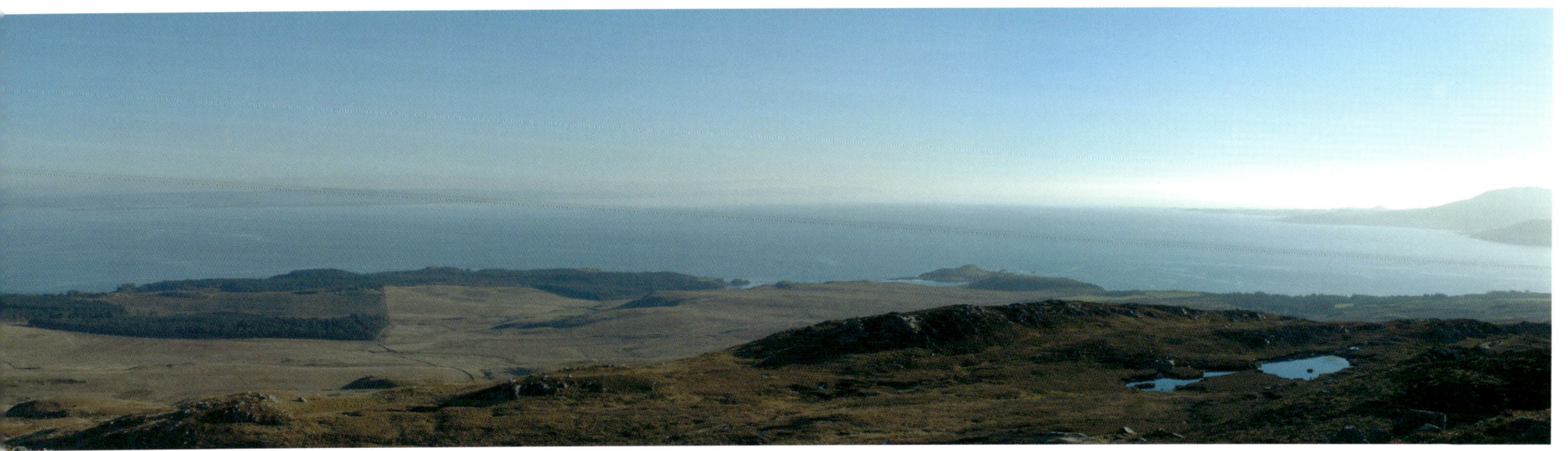

Keills

The cells or the churches

Keills (NR 5260 6830 approx.) is commonly associated with the ancient church of St. Ernán, Cille Earnadail. Although occasionally discussed by early Christian historians, Ernán is largely forgotten, as is the role of the small community that sprang up around the ancient church. According to the recollections of the Buies of Leargybreac, Keills was a political centre during the period of Somerled and the Lords of the Isles, in addition to the religious centre implied by its name.

The only land owned by MacDonald of the Isles (i.e. the Lord of the Isles) in Jura was Keills. The land of Keills included what is now the church glebe and marched (bounded: authur's note) with lands of Feolin (today's Feolin Farm: author's note). The old march dyke between Keills and Feolin, now between the glebe and Feolin, runs from the road up over the low hill behind.

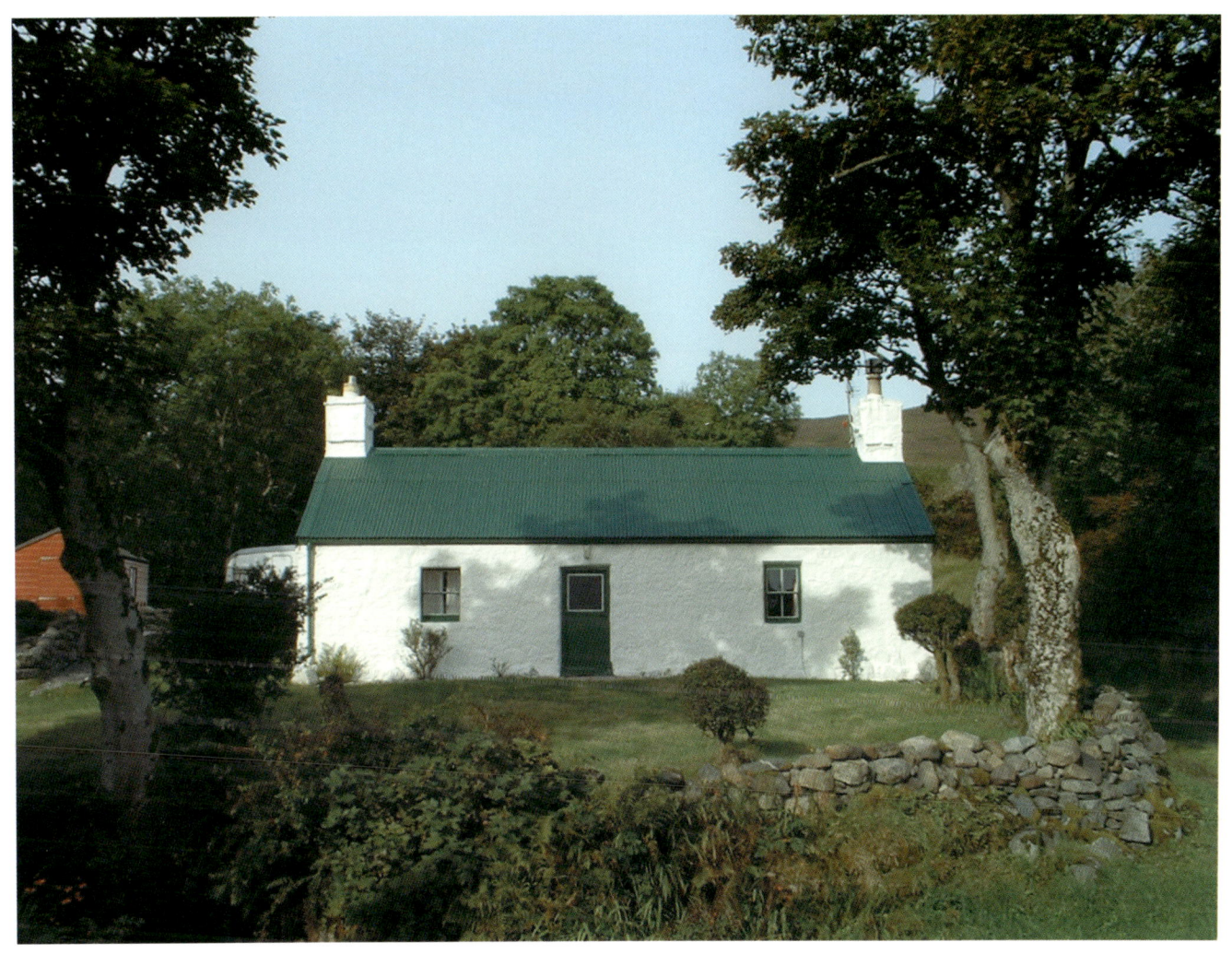

Craighouse

Tigh-na-craig

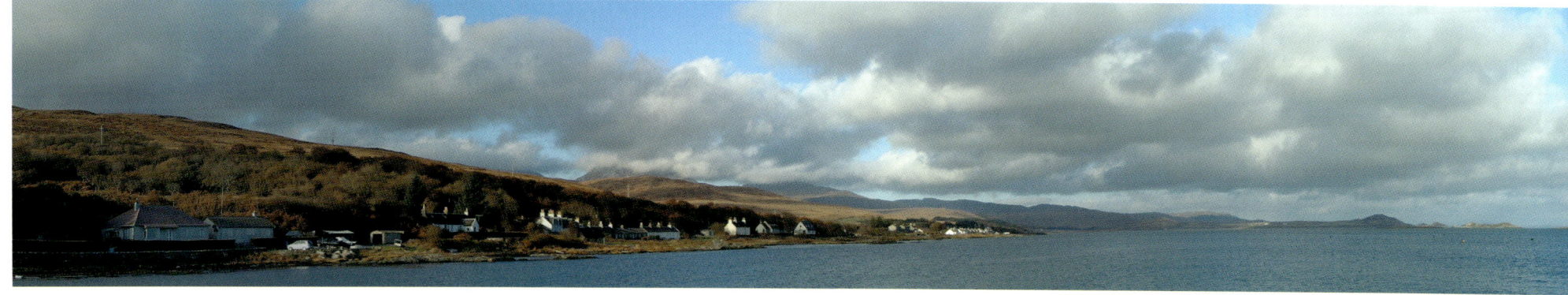

Craighouse (NR 5280 6730) has had many names and is one of the island's youngest communities. Its current name derives from the original name of the Jura Hotel, Tigh-na-craig [house on the rock], which began its life as one of Jura's four change houses that were built in the early 1800s to service travellers on the newly constructed road. Prior to that time, the community had the English appellation of "Milltown", due to the fact that a water-powered mill sat astride the *Allt Rogach* and ground meal for the surrounding area. This mill may be seen in William Daniell's famous line drawing/ engraving, which also gives a romantic view of Small Isles Bay and the present day Jura Stores. In this light a surviving "miller's tale" is provided.

The mill in Craighouse was run by the McIsaacs in the late 1790s. During that time Campbell of Jura became dissatisfied with McIsaac and replaced him with another man to do the mill work. Campbell's man wasn't popular with the local farmers and they asked for a meeting with the laird to discuss the situation. Campbell wasn't happy about this, of course, and immediately demanded to know what their complaint was about.

The head of the farmers said, "Well, this is the way of it, when we bring in our grain to be milled, we tie a knot in our sacks a certain way – and when we come back, the sacks are not tied the same way". Campbell of Jura was forced to save face and dismiss his man and replace him with McIsaac.

Campbell's miller couldn't tie his knots the same way as the farmers, which they knew the laird would recognise as their way of saying that he was stealing their meal.

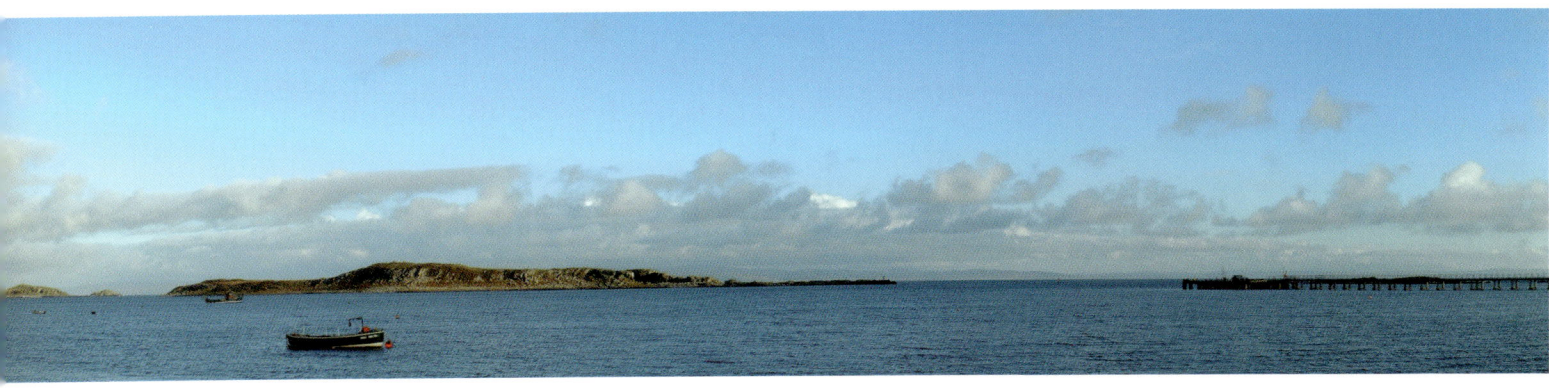

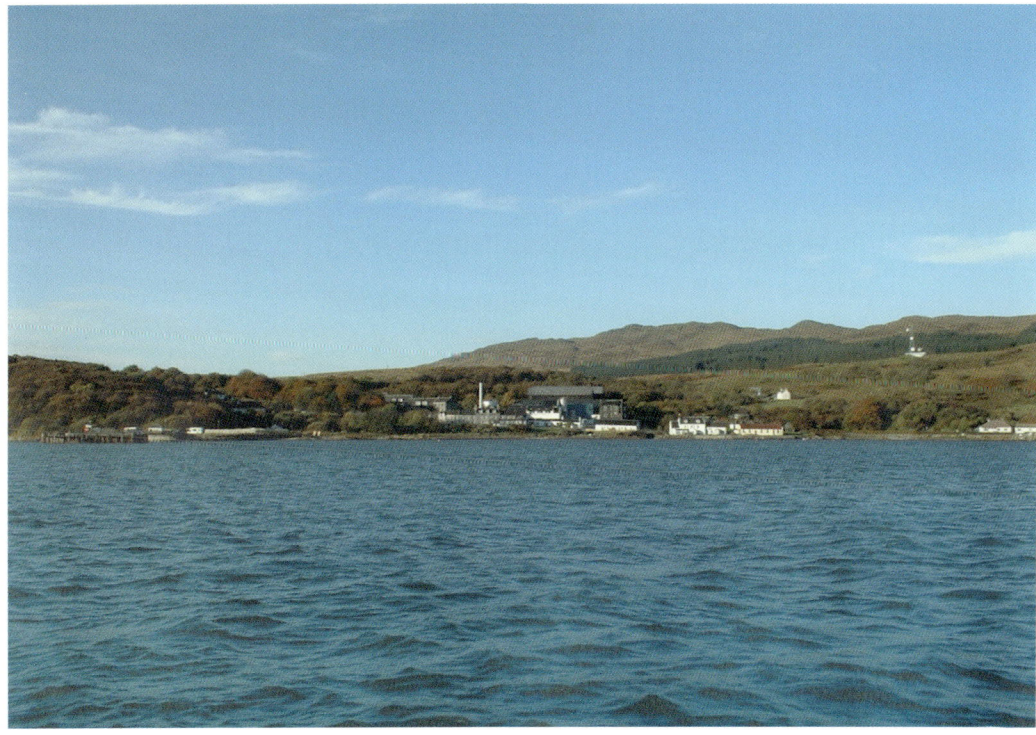

Sannaig

The sandy bay, from the Norse words, "san-vik"

Sannaig has a long history as the "political" capital of Jura. Earliest documents refer to the (albeit temporary) presence of Vikings, the MacDonalds during the Lords of the Isles period and, of course, the Campbells of Jura. Sannaig had several attractions: three natural and perfectly formed shallow bays below, one named Port na Birlinn [Port of the War Galley]; the best agricultural land in Jura; and proximity to the Sound of Islay, the natural highway up and down the west of Scotland.

Sannaig must have also been the place where justice was meted out. According to local legend, a long stone called Croic Mhic 'ille-raibhaich rested on two rocks at Sannaig shore; old *Dìurachs* [natives of Jura] could remember the halter, or *an gad*, still hanging from the gallows. This stone structure has since collapsed, making it untraceable, but the most likely area would be on the far side of Tràigh Bhàn Bheag, or "the little white beach", surely an ironic last sight for a condemned man.

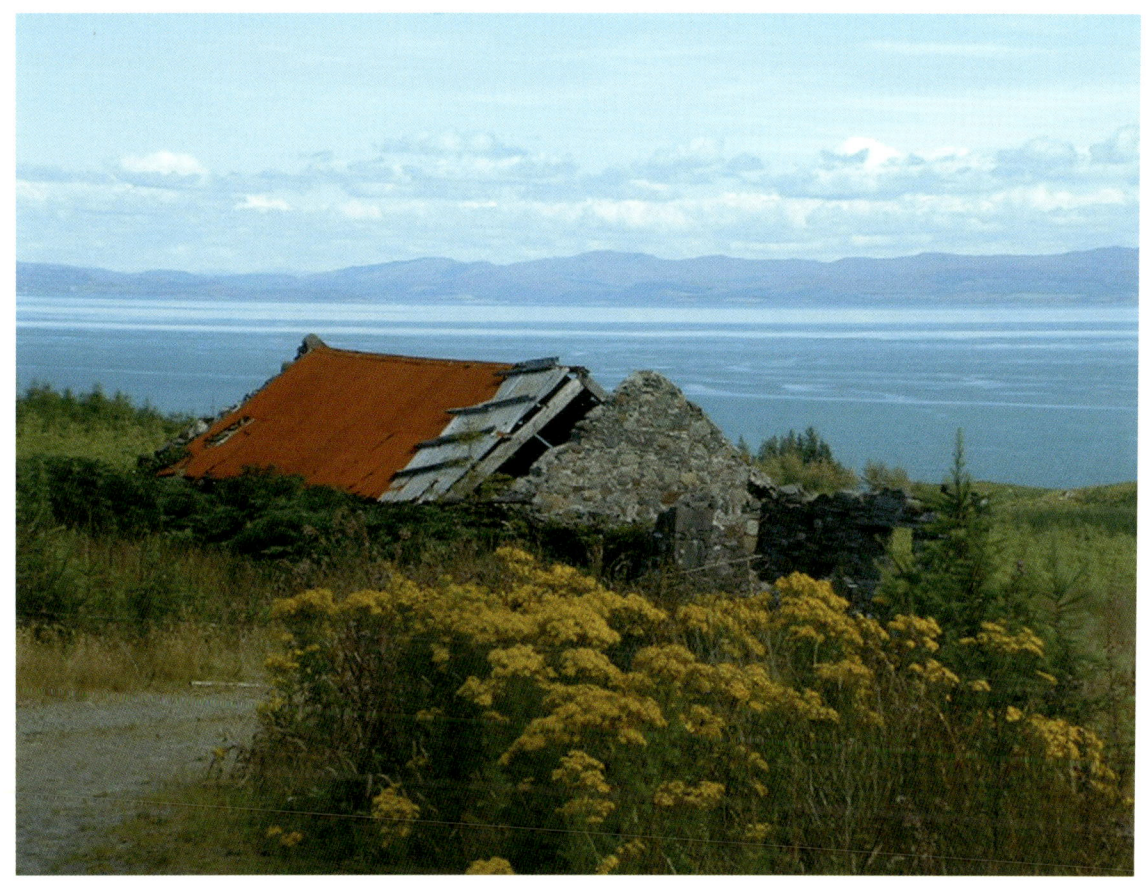

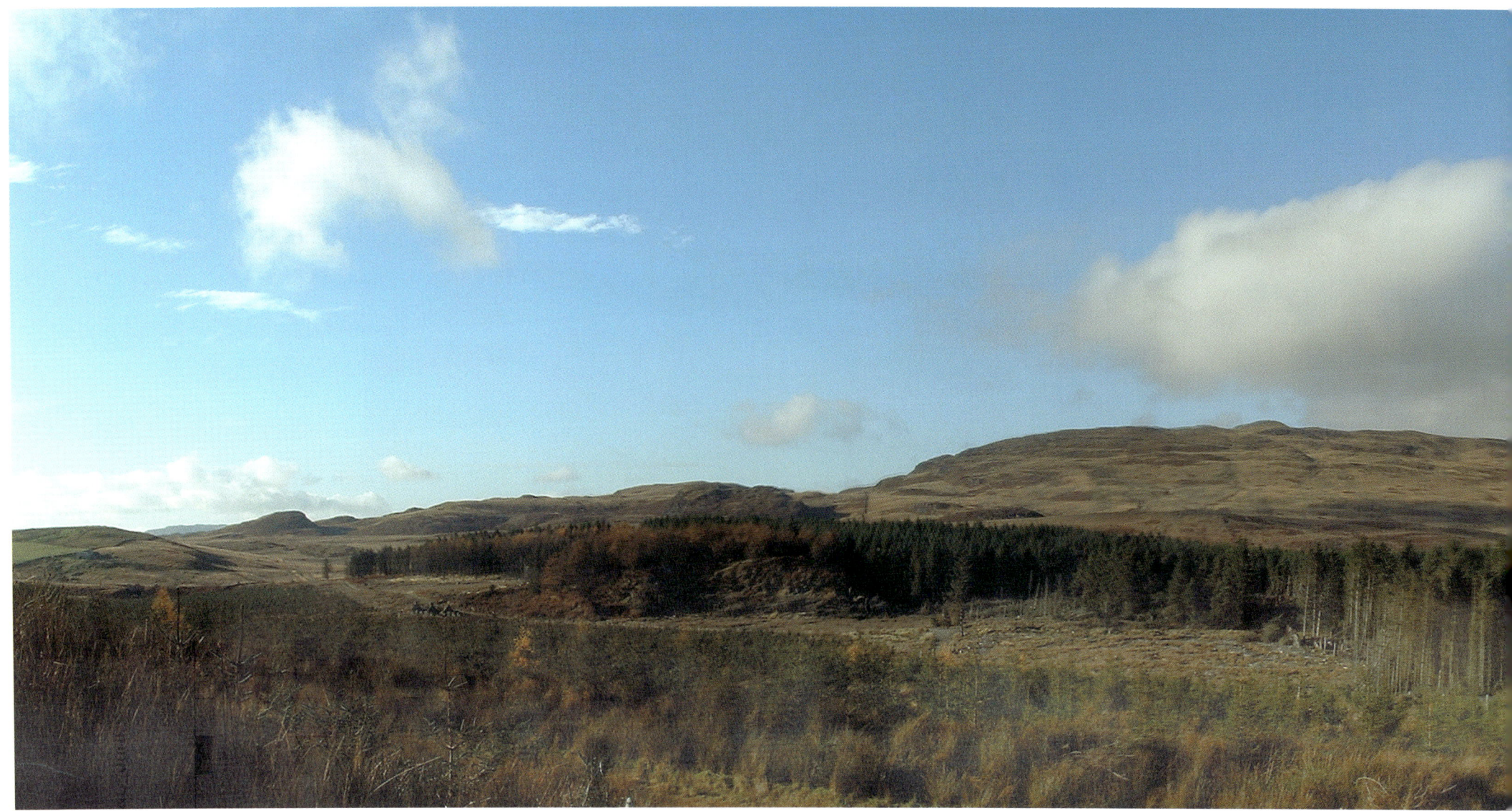

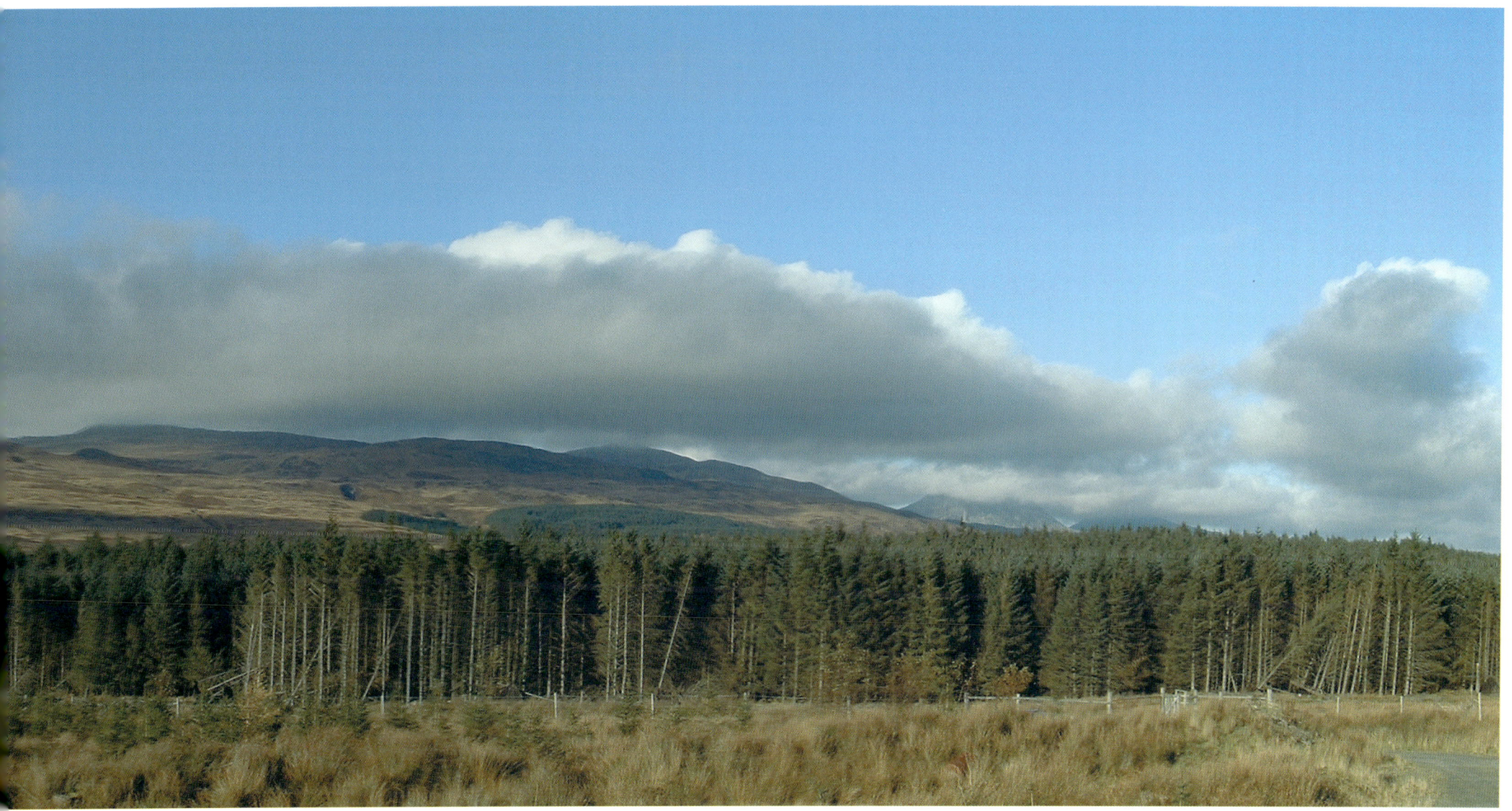

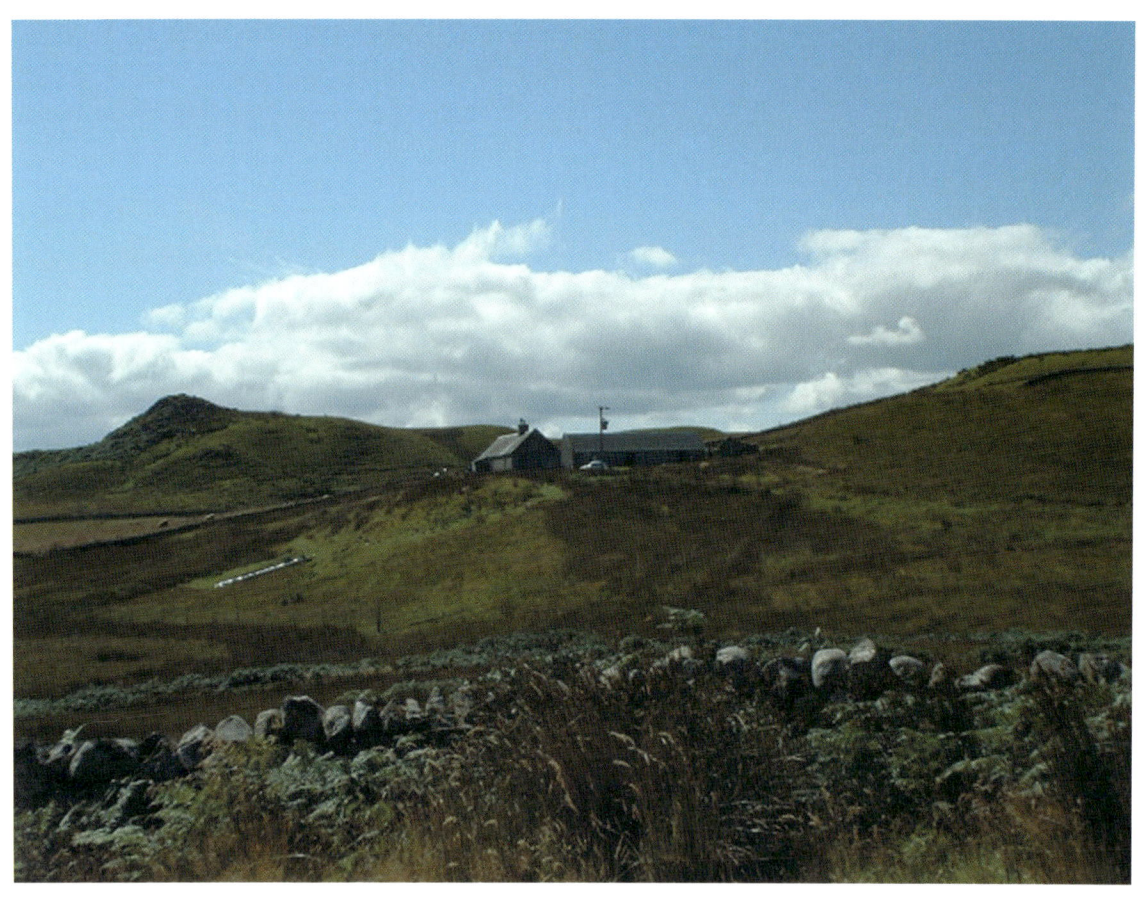

Strone

The headland

Today Strone (NR 5050 6440 approx.) is occupied by one lone house, but it was once the centre of some of Jura's most productive agricultural fields. As was common in the Gaelic world, fields would be left to lie fallow for a few years to rest the soil and give it time to renew, both naturally and through man's assistance with fertilisers such as seaweed and manure. Then, as now, disagreements would break out over farmland; the following story describes how one enclosure, near Strone, came to be known as Achadh na h-iorgail [Field of the quarrel].

The field had lain fallow as long as anyone in the community could remember and so it was decided to use it again to grow crops. The whole community pitched in to prepare the field for the planting of a corn crop, which was done, and then the sowing was done as well.

The corn grew quickly and ripened. Soon it was ready to be harvested and, on a day agreed on by all, they gathered to begin the harvest. However, an argument soon broke out about who had contributed most in preparing the field and who should get the greater share of the crop. The argument soon reached a blood rage and people had to be separated from each other; bloodshed was feared.

That evening the men of each household prepared not for a harvest the next day but for a battle, and sharpened their knives. The argument would be settled with the rise of the sun.

A *cailleach* [old woman] had watched and listened to the whole affair and feared there would be a great tragedy. All through the night she thought and worried about how to end the disagreement. Late, in the deepest moments of the night, when the whole community was asleep, even the men who had been preparing for battle, the old woman slipped away. No one saw her leave, where she went, or what she did.

At sunrise the next day, the men from each household armed themselves for battle and strode towards the field. As they approached they were stunned into silence – for instead of a field of gold, before them lay a field of black stubble. A fire during the night had consumed the entire field.

It was many years before anyone discovered the truth behind how the quarrel was ended by the old woman of Strone.

Brosdale

The Broad Dale

The MacIans, a cadet house of the MacDonalds of Ardnamurchan, had arrived on Jura during the early 1500s and settled at Brosdale. On one occasion they captured a Buie and tied him up, leaving him on the summit of Crackaig Hill. A MacIan follower was then sent to inform Buie of Jura. Buie, greatly enraged, gathered up his men and set off to rescue his kinsman. One of the MacIans, upon hearing that Buie was coming, said, "I suppose Buie will settle the dispute between us and then we'll have to set the fellow free".

Another of the MacIans, who became greatly enraged upon hearing this comment, pulled out his *sgian dhu* [dirk] and plunged it into the chest of the helpless prisoner. Buie of Jura, along with his followers, flew into a blood rage and slew every male MacIan on the island, thus virtually blotting out the name on Jura. The spot where the MacIans were buried is marked by stones, still pointed out at Brosdale, on the right bank of the Strone burn, not far from the beach.

Although this story is attributed to Brosdale, Cladh Chlainn Iain (the place where the MacIans are buried), does indeed lie on the right bank of the Abhainn na Sròine, [River of the Headland] at NR 5059 6310 approx. where it drains into *Poll a' Cheo* [Misty Bay].

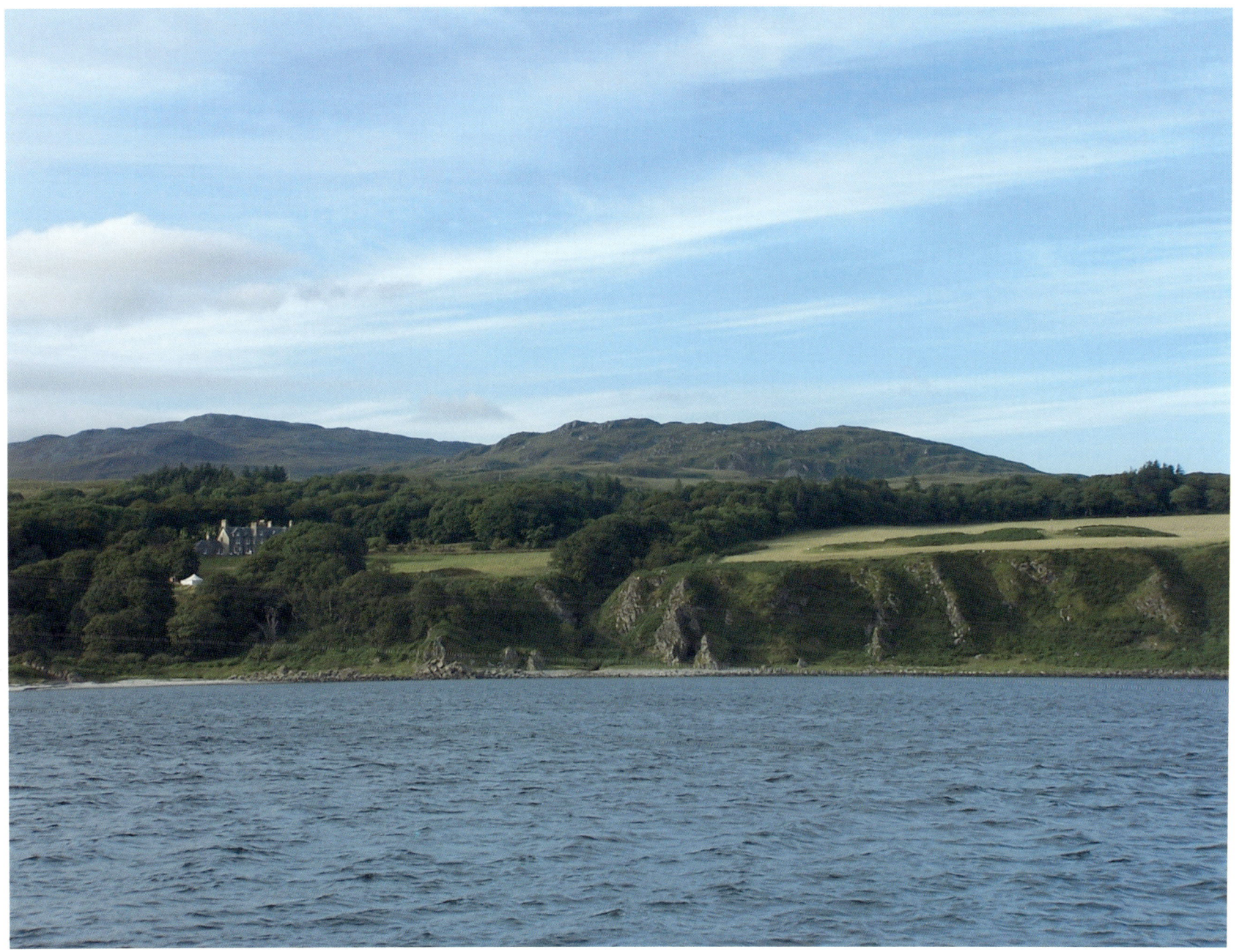

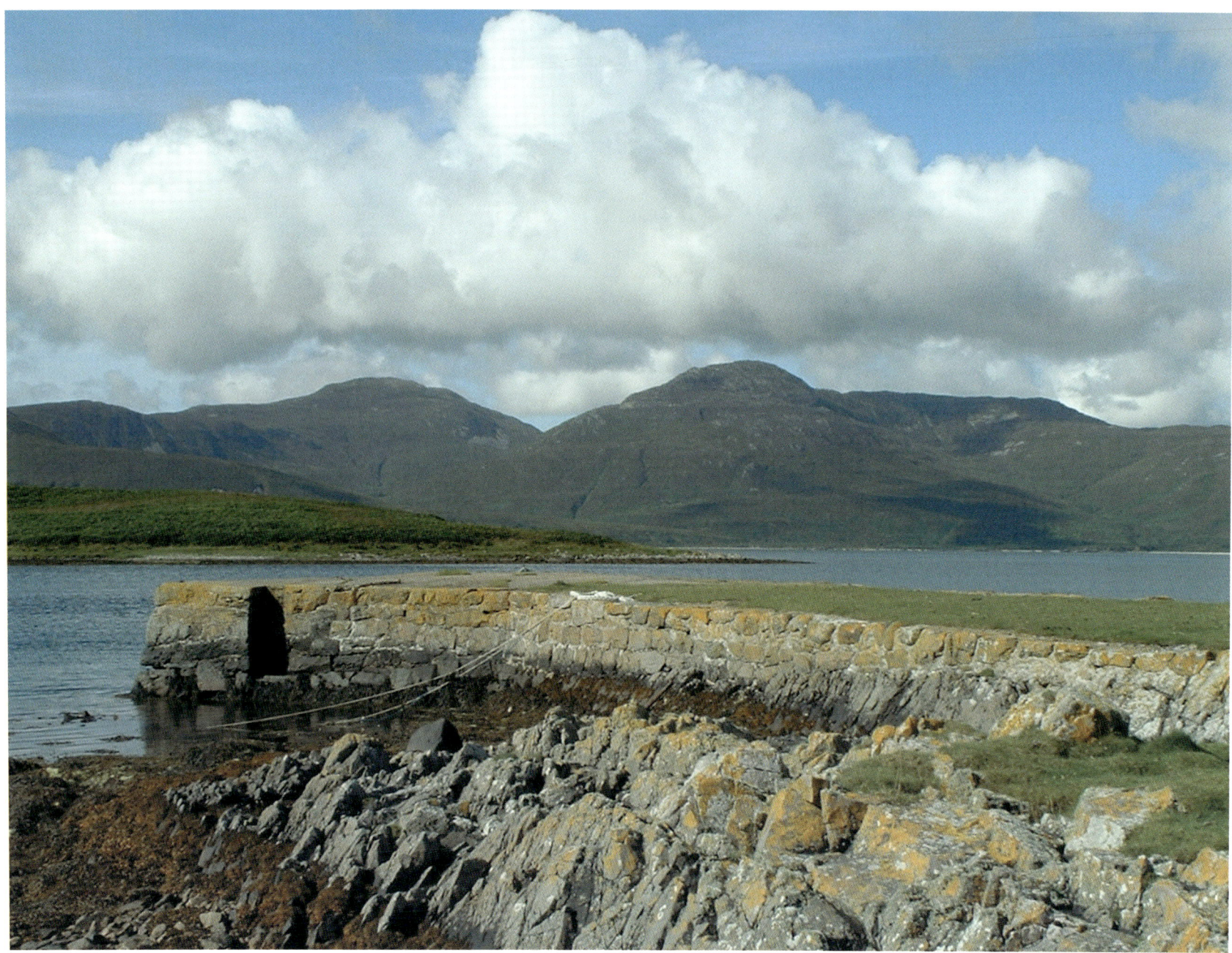

Ardfin

The high end of the island

Many stories are told about the changeover in the control of Jura which happened during the period when the MacDonalds, or Lords of the Isles, were in collapse on nearby Islay. The story told below gives a unique perspective on these times at Ardfin (NR 4780 6370) from the point of view of the Buies, a sept of the MacDonalds. The Campbells of Jura were the representatives of the Campbells of Craignish (in Knapdale on the mainland) and until a comparatively recent time designated "of Craignish and Jura". The local tradition as to how the Campbells of Jura gained goes as follows:

MacDonald of Jura had his house at Ardfin and said to Campbell of Craignish that as long as he could keep him out of his house at Ardfin he would keep his lands in Jura from him. "If I can get into your house," said Campbell, "will you give up the place to me?" MacDonald replied, "If you can get into my house I will let you have Jura to yourself". MacDonald secured his doors and windows so that it seemed impossible to obtain an entrance by any means – and promptly went from his home that day about his business. Campbell, coming to the house, attempted to gain entry by window and door, but to no avail; but then spying that the smoke hole was quite large he had himself hoisted onto the roof by one of his followers. Lowering himself through the smoke hole carefully he managed to gain his feet inside without burns or being choked by smoke. When MacDonald came home at the end of the day and let himself into his house he found Campbell of Craignish seated in his chair by his fire. MacDonald left Jura that day and never returned, thus leaving Jura to the Campbells.

Claig Castle

The stone castle

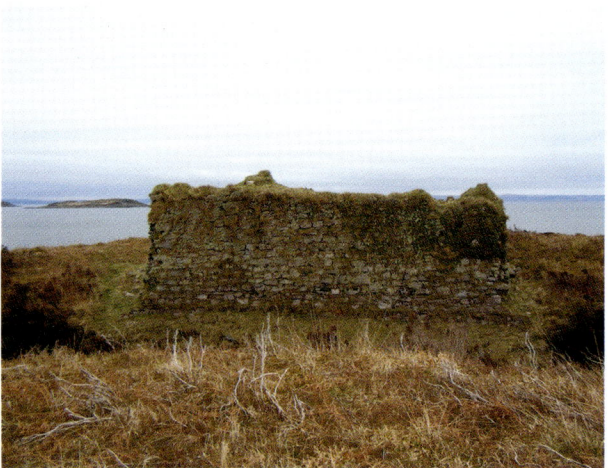

Claig Castle (NR 4700 6270) is located on Am Fraoch Eilean, a small island off the south-west coast of Jura. Its most impressive feature from a distance is its great natural trench, which appears almost to cut the island in two. Located on the very edge of this precipice, and on the south side of the island, is the imposing castle, labelled by archaeologists as a "fortified house". The walls of the structure are on average three metres thick and it once had a second storey. The construction of the fortification is impressive and it appears to have been built of stone quarried from Arran. It has been suggested that the castle was built during the early 13th century, but definitive proof is lacking. At any rate, the castle is never known to have been successfully captured while the MacDonalds of the Isles held sway; it is assumed that it was manned by *Dìurachs* [natives of Jura]. The castle was essentially the "Gibraltar of the Hebrides" as control of the Sound of Islay meant control of the west coast of Scotland to a large degree; anyone daring to sail in the open Atlantic Ocean west of Islay faced dangerous reefs. The fame of the castle exceeds even that of the Hebrides; when Angus Og, Lord of the Isles, led the men alongside Robert the Bruce at the Battle of Bannockburn in 1314, their war cry was, "AM FRAOCH EILEAN!" [For my heather isle!].

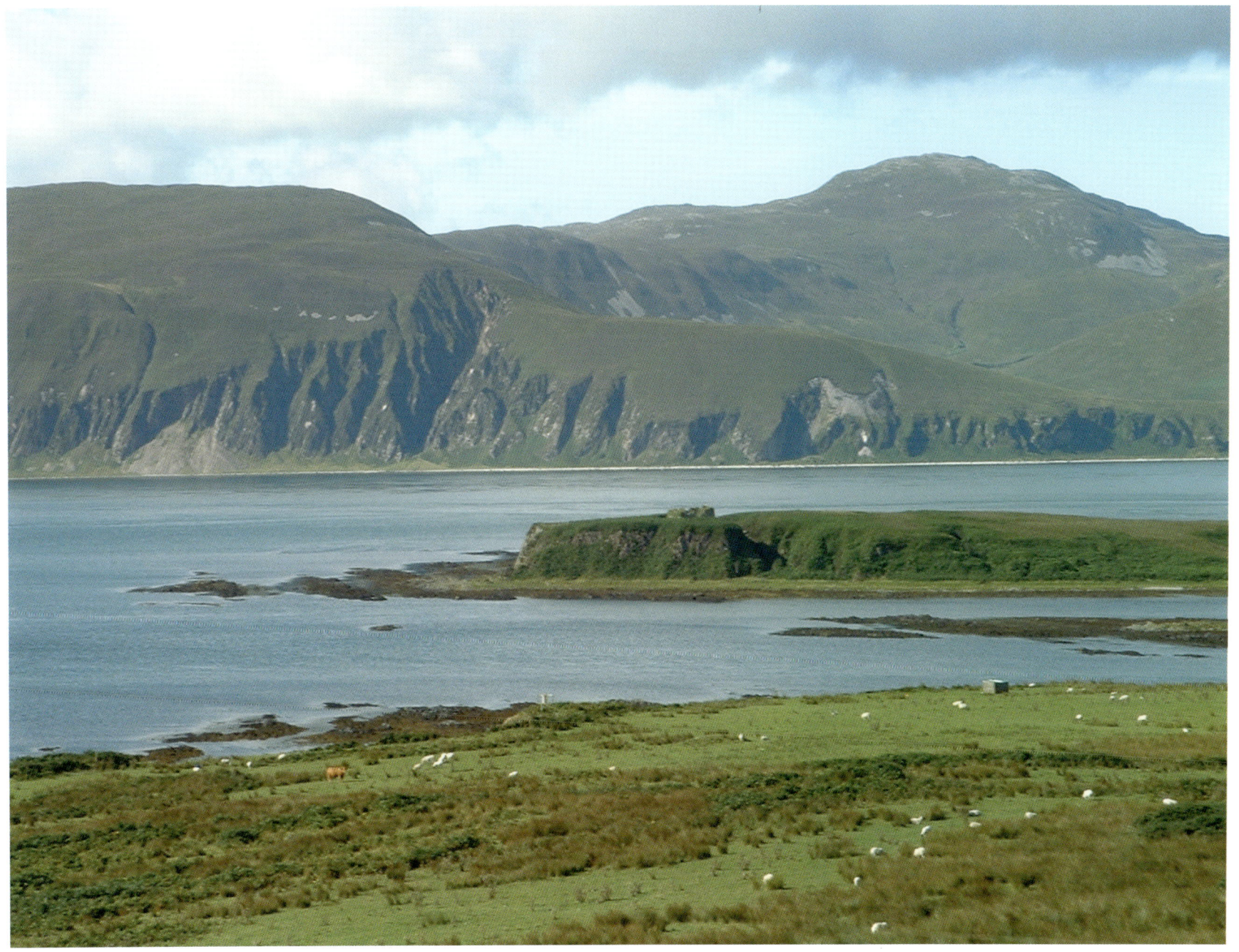

Camas an Staca

The bay of the stone column

Camas an Staca (NR 4620 6420) is well-known for its large standing stone, the age of which is uncertain. Virtually unknown today, however, is the story of Jura's "cannibal" *cailleach* [old woman] and her lair near the standing stone.

The *cailleach*, when the opportunity appeared, carried away children from the shielings and devoured them. Once a man and his sons who had been fishing in the Sound of Islay took shelter for the night in the Uamh Ruadh below Camas an Staca. As they began to settle in for the night the *cailleach* appeared and joined their company, without them knowing who she was, of course. Some of the young men then went out to bring in additional supplies of fish for the night's supper and some more fuel for the cooking fire. The *cailleach* made some excuse to absent her self as well. As the young men were a long time gone, their brothers went out to search for them to see what was detaining them. When they too did not return, the father rushed out to search for them all. Finding the *cailleach* attempting to drag one of his young sons away, the father secured his safety while shouting for the rest of his sons to push out their fishing boat. The *cailleach* rushed onto the beach and screamed for them to let her have the youngest, fattest boy and she would be content.

The *cailleach* of Camas an Staca's fortunes are concluded at Daimh Sgeir…

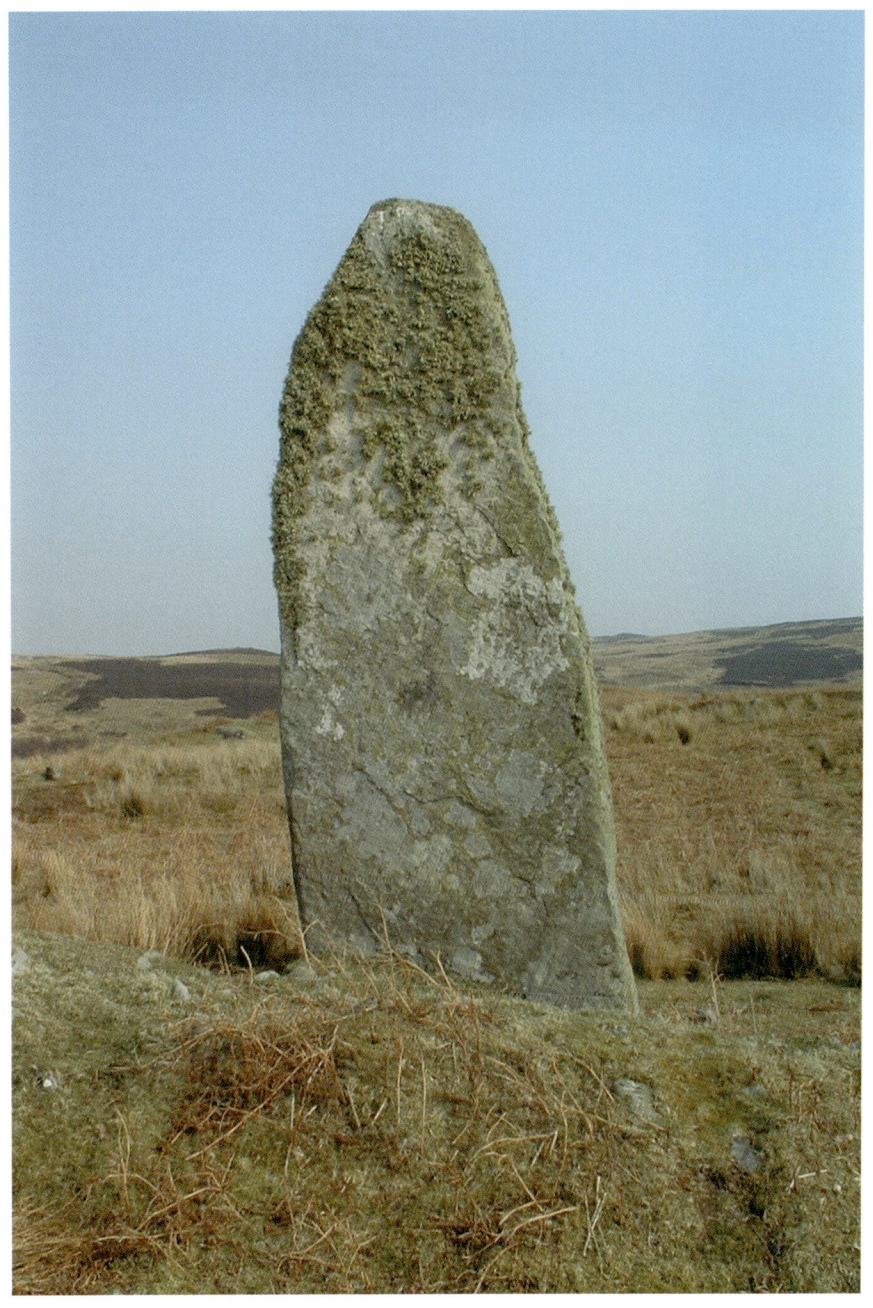

Daimh-sgeir

The skerry of the deer

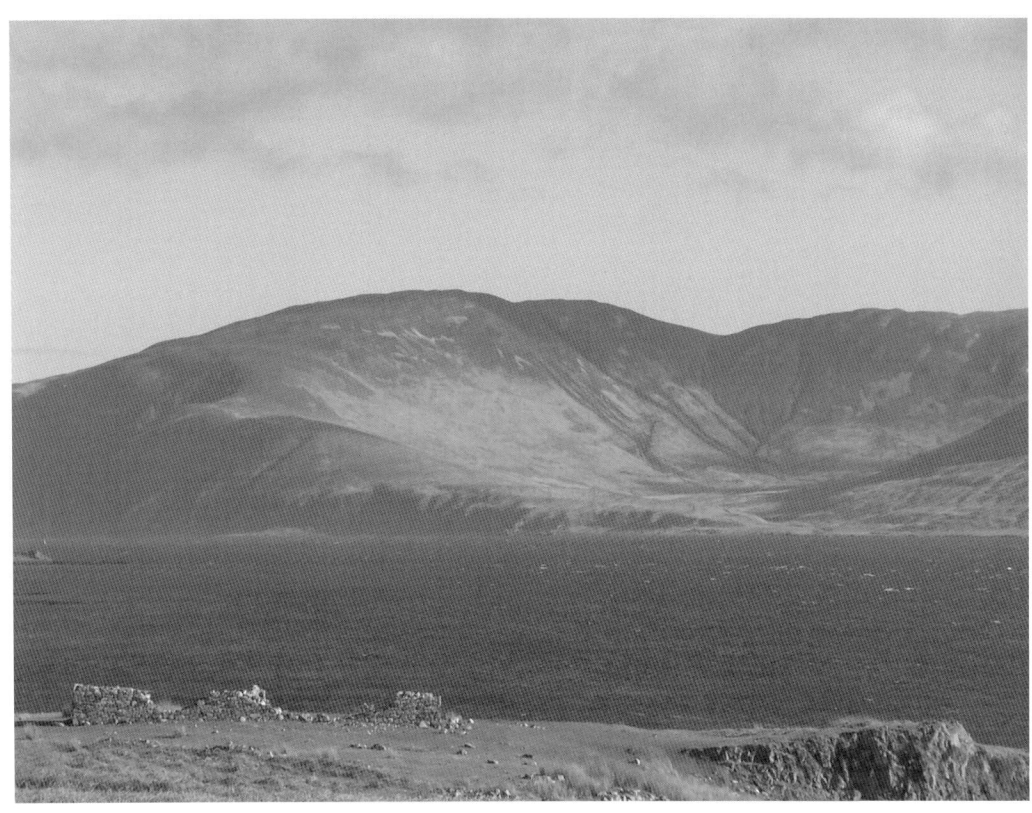

Daimh Sgeir (NR 4430 6720) was inhabited until the 1930s and is known to have been the abode of the last boat builders of south Jura during the 1800s. What is virtually unknown today is its reputation as the resting place of the "cannibal" *cailleach* [old woman] of Camas Staca. Here then is the conclusion of the career of the *cailleach* who apparently terrorised south Jura and, as usual in the island's history, it was a Mac 'ille-bhuidhe or Buie who delivered Highland justice.

The son of Mac 'ille-bhuidhe (Buie), like his father, was renowned for being a crack shot with either gun or bow and arrow. Travelling along the south-west coast of Jura young Mac 'ille-bhuidhe caught sight of the *cailleach* in the little glen of Daimh-sgeir. Putting his gun to his shoulder he fired his gun at the *cailleach* and broke her leg. The *cailleach* screamed and the young Mac 'ille-bhuidhe fired again, this time killing her. The *cailleach* was buried on the north side of the Abhainn an Daimh-sgeir and her grave can still be traced there.

The grave of the *cailleach* of Camas an Staca can indeed still be seen today, just a few hundred metres up the small glen from the stone bridge at Daimh-sgeir, exactly as described.

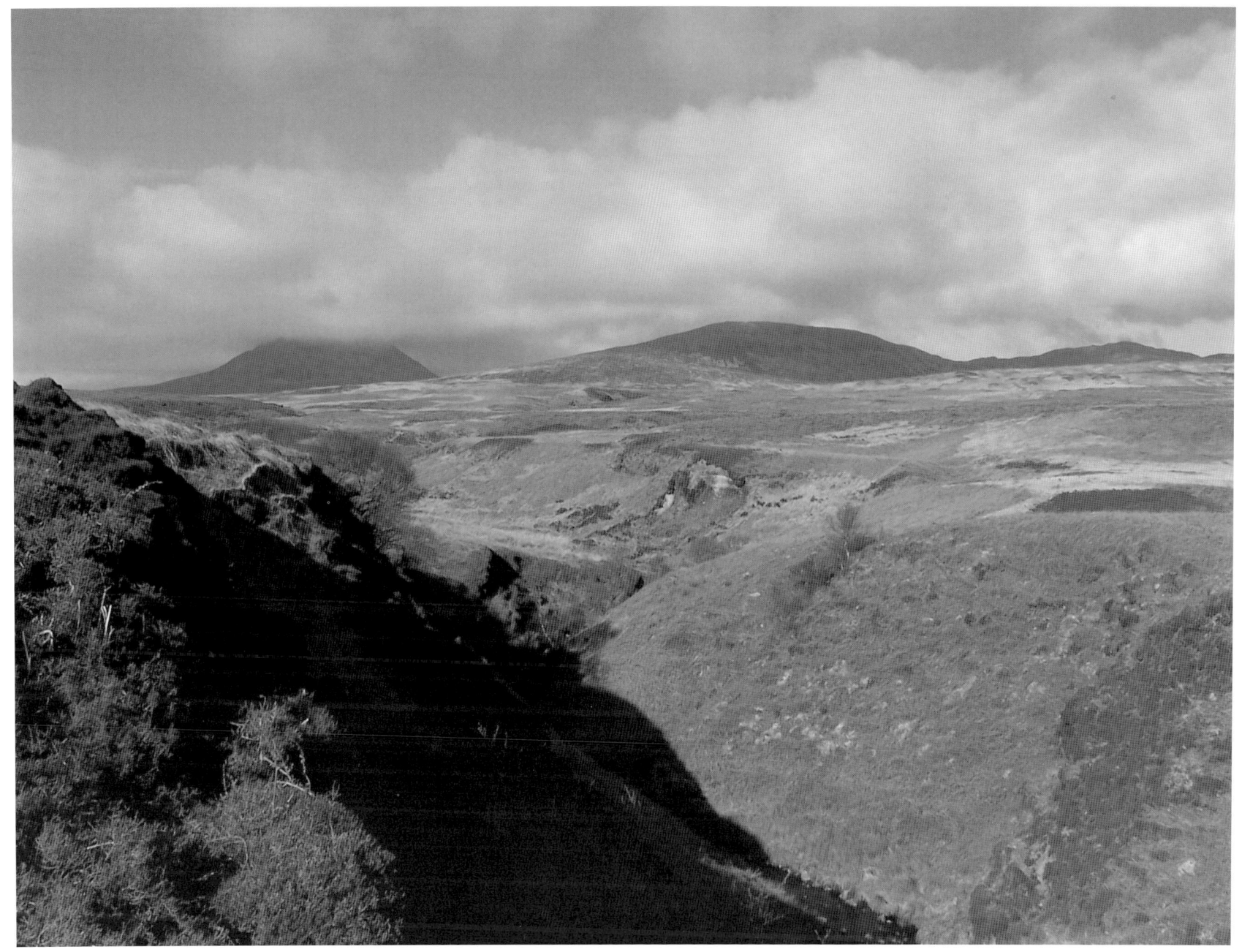

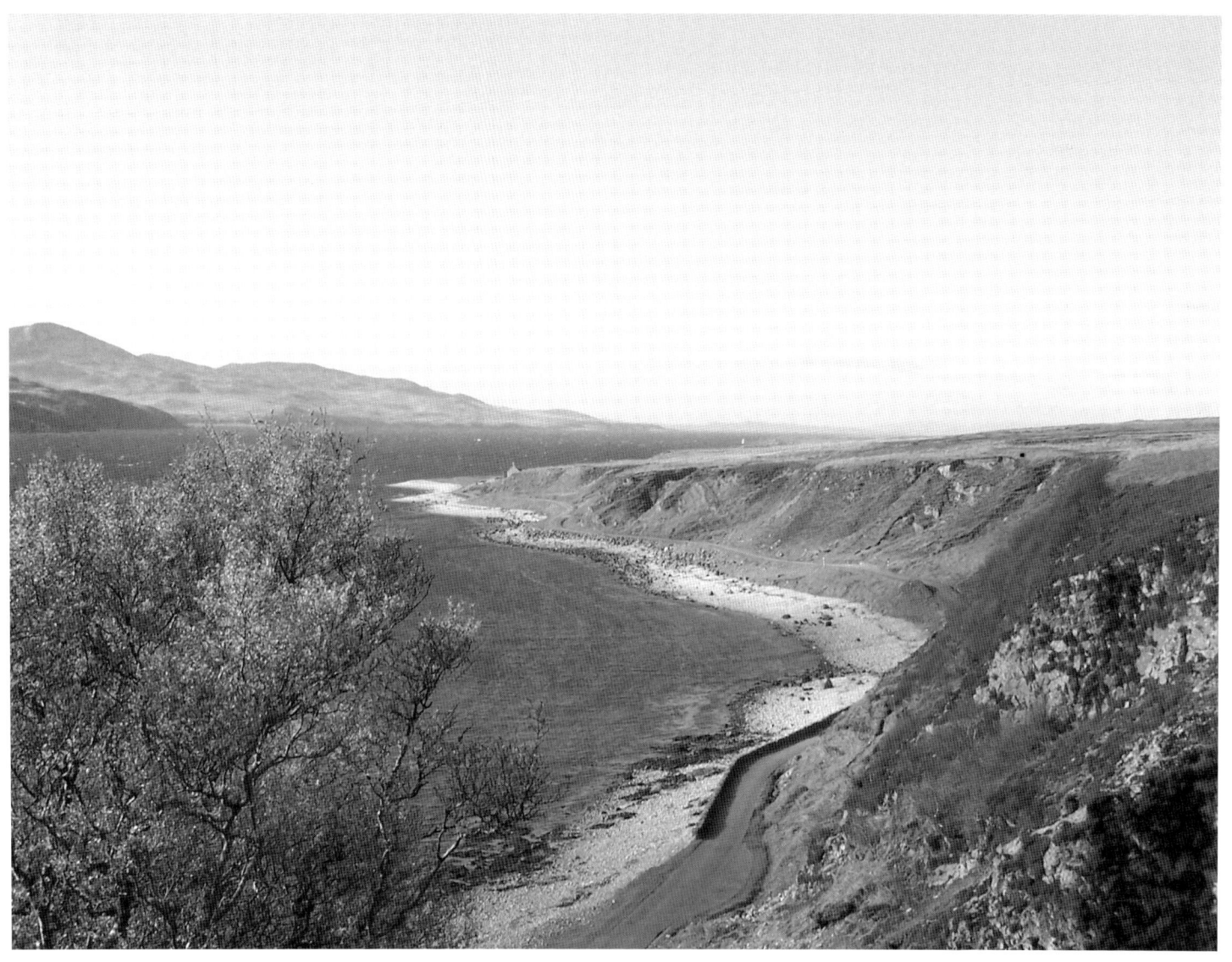

Feolin Ferry

The seagull ferry

As the arrival and departure point for many on the island, Feolin Ferry (NR 4410 6910 approx.) is perhaps an appropriate place to present Jura's unofficial "anthem", which expresses a Diurach's longing for home. The poetic and musical skills of Jura's people have not diminished with time.

Crossing to Jura

Soon I'll cross to Jura isle
Where my dearest ones are dwelling,
Mother waits to welcome me,
Mine's a joy beyond all telling.

Chorus:
I shall sail across the Sound,
I shall sail across the Ferry,
To my native isle I'm bound,
Braving wind and wave and skerry.

Sailing swiftly toward the lea,
Strong brown hand upon the tiller,
Now my father's form I see,
Wind and tide can hold no terror.

Chorus:

Flesh of deer will hill provide,
Fresh-run salmon shall the river,
Shy grey-hen and mallard wild,
To my gun will fall as ever.

Chorus:

Calm delight my heart shall warm
Light my step to Lussa-given,
Gaelic speech my ear shall charm,
Dearest isle under Heaven.

Chorus:

By Neil Shaw of Jura

Null thar an Aiseig

Fonn: Theid mi null gu tir mo rùin,
Theid mi null thar an aiseig,
Theid mi null gu tir mo rùin,
S'mòr mo shunnd a' tilleadh dhachaidh

Theid mi null ann thar a chaoil,
Far a'bheil mo dhaoin a fanachd,
Gheibh mì fàillt bo'm mhàthair chaoin,
'Nuair bu mhaoth mi 's I rinn m'altruinn,

Ch mi 'm bàta fo a siuil,
A tighinn dlùth do na chala,
Chi mi m'athair aig an stiùir,
Cha bhi cùram orm bho'n chas-shruth.

As a' bheinn gun toir mi fiadh,
Gheibh mi iasg as an Abhainn,
Le mo ghunna mar is miann,
Gheibh mi liath-chearc is lacha.

Bidh mo chridhe leum le mùirn,
'S mòr mo shunnd is chan airsneul,
Chan 'eil coiemas tir mo rùin
Ann an dùthaich eil' air thalamh.

Inver

The head of the sea loch

Several very early stories mention Inver as the place where Vikings or Norse raiding parties landed, and it certainly features in later tales of raids and counter raids during the clan period. In front of Inver, just metres from the Sound of Islay, is the enigmatically named Lochan Iasgaich [Shallow Loch of the Young Heroes], perhaps referring to some battle where a group of young men fought valiantly against overwhelming odds. Here is a local story that is not only related orally but also is recorded in the written *Chronicles of Craignish*:

After the final collapse of the Lords of the Isles in the late 1400s and early 1500s, the western half of Islay was granted to the MacLeans of Duart by the Scottish Crown. The MacDonalds who remained on Islay did not hold with the idea that their ancient lands could be taken from them and did not honour the Crown's decree. The MacLeans of Duart did not press their claim for the lands on Islay at first, but the next generation did, for in 1585 an event on Jura caused the feud between the MacLeans and MacDonalds to explode into bloody conflict.

Donald Gorm MacDonald of the House of Sleat was travelling by sea to pay a visit to his cousin, Angus MacDonald of Dunyveg, Islay, when contrary sea conditions forced his vessel to come ashore on Jura, and more importantly in an area of the island controlled by the MacLeans. While making camp on Jura another vessel landed not too far from the MacDonald party; this boating party was also from Sleat, but contained MacDonalds who were under a sentence of outlawry from Donald Gorm and so hated the Sleat chief. The two outlawed Sleat men leading the party were Hugh Gillespie and Alexander MacDonald. These men were known to have been plotting the downfall of the Sleat

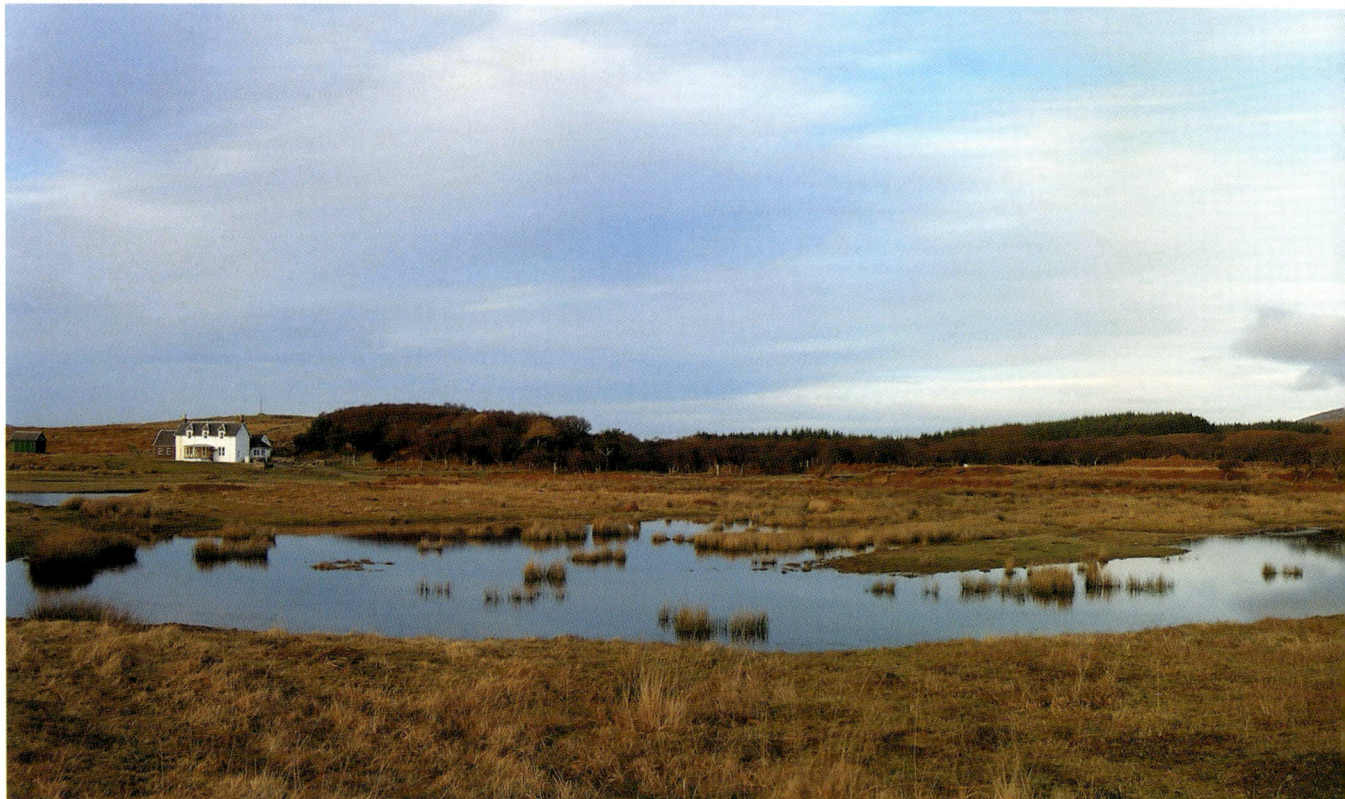

chief and had followed his voyage with an eye to causing trouble with the MacLeans.

The next night Gillespie and MacDonald with their outlawed band of men stole a number of cattle from the MacLean holdings nearby and, as soon as the weather calmed, made away under sail. Their plot to foment trouble for Donald Gorm succeeded, for the MacLeans, while not openly in arms against any MacDonalds at the time, had seen the landing of the Sleat chief's men and immediately suspected them. The next day the unsuspecting Sleat chief and his party moved further south along the western Jura coast to Inver beneath Cnocbreac and made camp for the night. That evening they were ambushed by a party of MacLean men lead by Lachlan

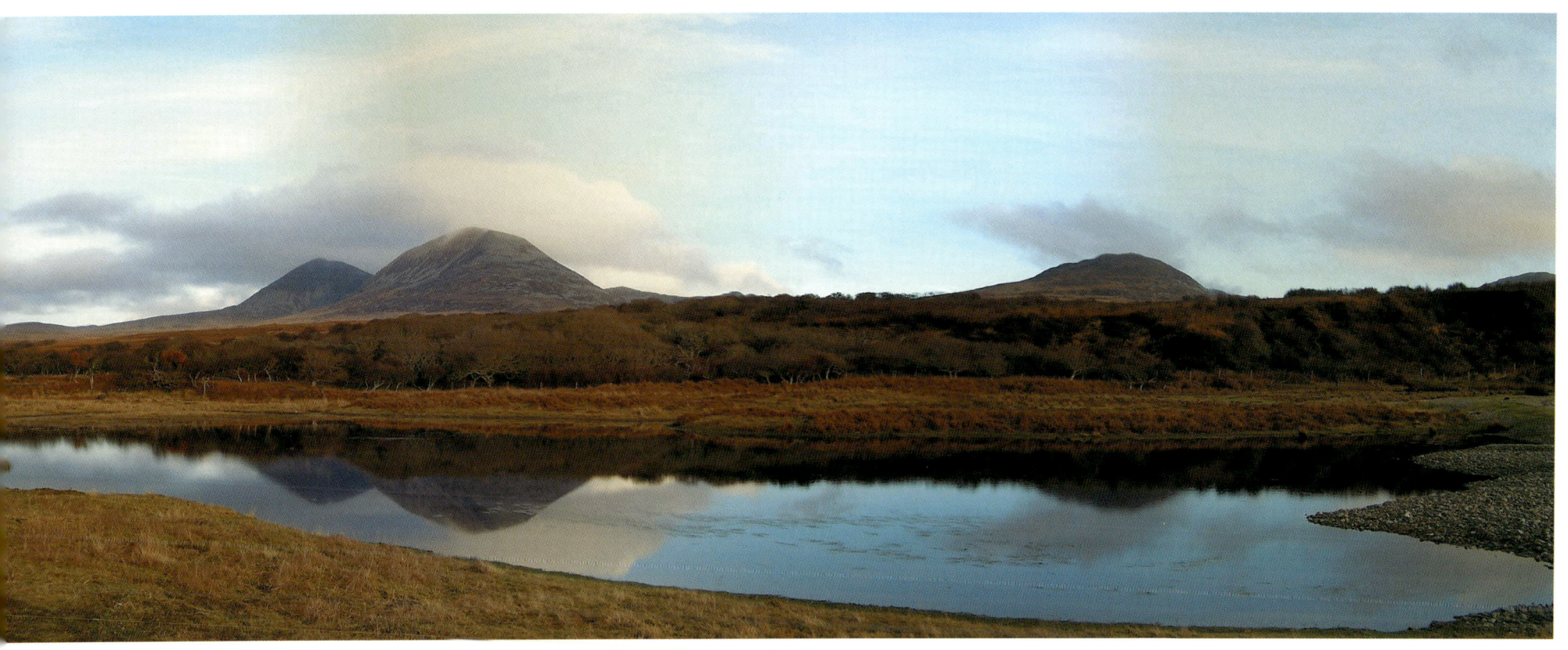

Mór. Sixty of Donald Gorm's men from Sleat were killed.

Donald Gorm and a few of his men escaped only because they had followed the time-tested rule of sleeping that night aboard their vessel, which lay offshore of Inver (today's Whitfarland Bay: author's note).

Cnocbreac

The speckled hill or hill of broken ground

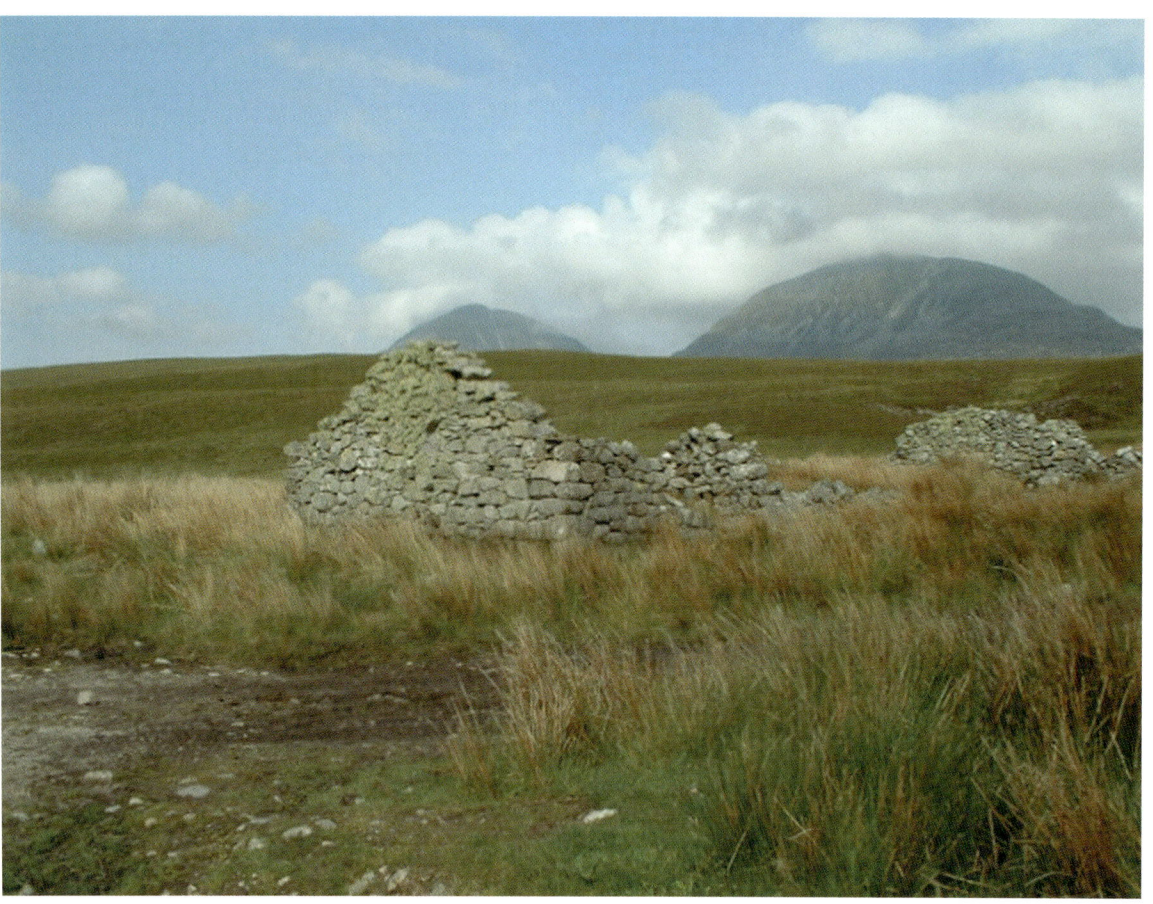

Cnocbreac (NR 4480 7310 approx.) may be the only settlement on Jura to have been cleared of its inhabitants. Allegedly, one of its community poached a salmon from the Abhainn a' Chnuic Bhric, thus enraging Campbell of Jura. His factor was instructed to remove all the residents, most of whom, according to oral history, moved to Islay. It was later proved to Campbell that the alleged poaching never occurred and the laird invited the inhabitants to return, but that they all refused. While census records can only partly support this oral legend of Cnocbreac, they do show a very small population by 1851 and virtually none since, a strange coincidence for one of the richest landscapes in the west of Jura. Oral history tells of numerous fairy hills around Shian and to the west of Tarbert, particularly at Cnocbreac; perhaps these are not fairies at Cnocbreac but the ghosts of past inhabitants.

Uamh Da Dhoruis

The Cave of Two Doors

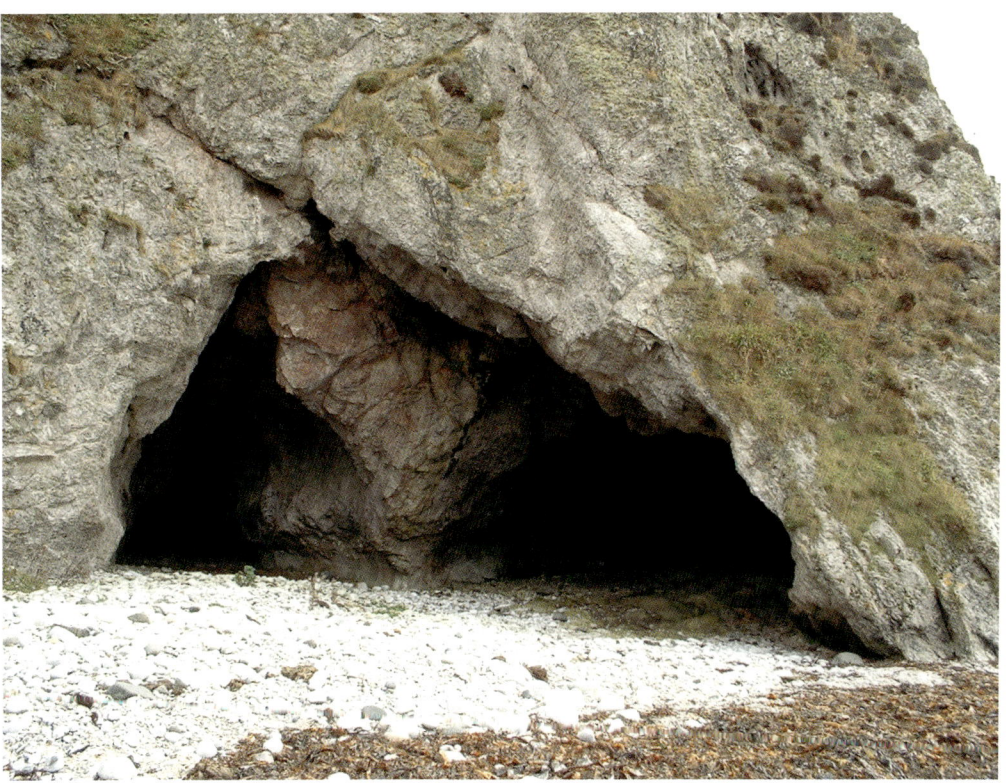

Among the surnames long associated with Jura, such as Buie and Shaw, are the Mac 'ille-riabhaich, better known today as the Darrochs.

According to legend, one of the more colourful Darrochs used to imprison men, women and children in Uamh Da Dhoruis, located on the west coast of Jura (NR 4460 7460 approx.). These would be people he had captured from Colonsay, Islay and even Jura. He would heap heather and wood or anything he could find at both ends of the openings to the cave, set fire to the heaps of fuel, and then suffocate all his prisoners.

Even today Uamh Da Dhoruis shows the effects of fire in certain portions of its roof and entrances. Only archaeological investigation may be able to reveal whether this is merely evidence of past fishermen and present day backpackers, or of ancient Highland justice.

The Paps of Jura and Sgriob na Caillich

The breast-shaped mountains of Jura and the old woman's scree

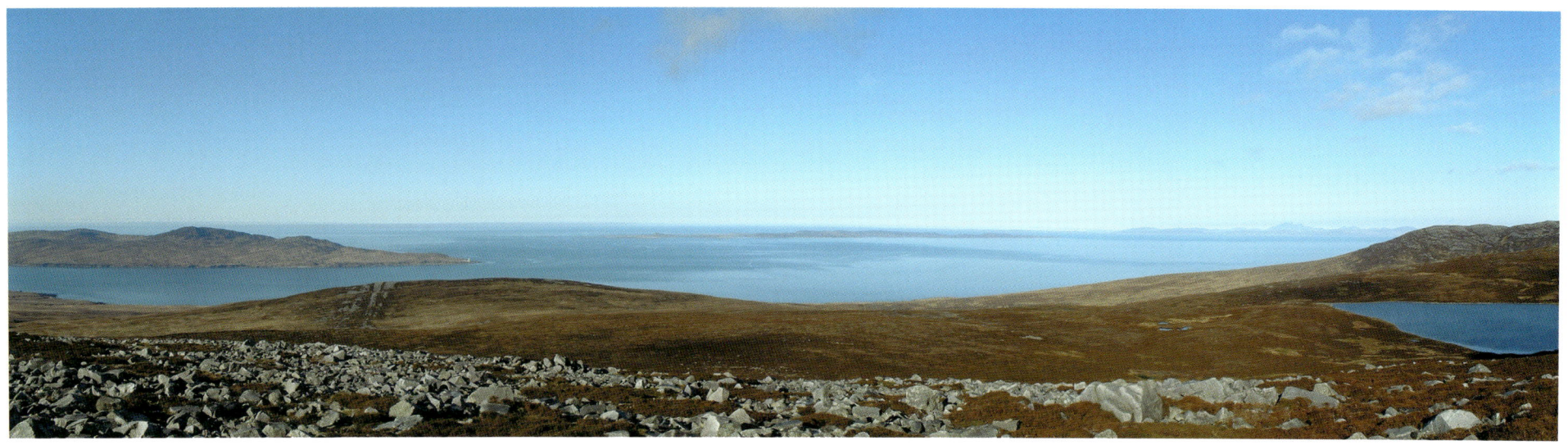

Many tales involve the Paps of Jura, but perhaps the oldest and most embellished concerns a *cailleach* [old woman] who lived on Beinn an Oir, the highest Pap of Jura.

The *cailleach* was a great, wild woman who made her home in a cave, the entrance of which is now unknown, near the summit of the mountain. Once, when standing on the summit, the *cailleach* wished to descend to the west side of Jura and, not knowing any other way, sat down on the slope, held out her feet straight in front and slid down. The Sgriob na Caillich (NR 4700 7680 approx.) is the remains of the track she left behind in her descent; it is visible today as a great stripe running down the western flank of Beinn an Oir.

Geologists attribute this feature to glacial debris suspended between two separate glaciers, the debris slowly settling onto the surface of Beinn an Oir's western side in a linear fashion over thousands of years. And the *cailleach*? All stories have a kernel of truth and numerous place names on Jura refer to the "cave of the old woman" or the "rock of the old woman"; it is likely that, at some point, a very old woman lived on Beinn an Oir.

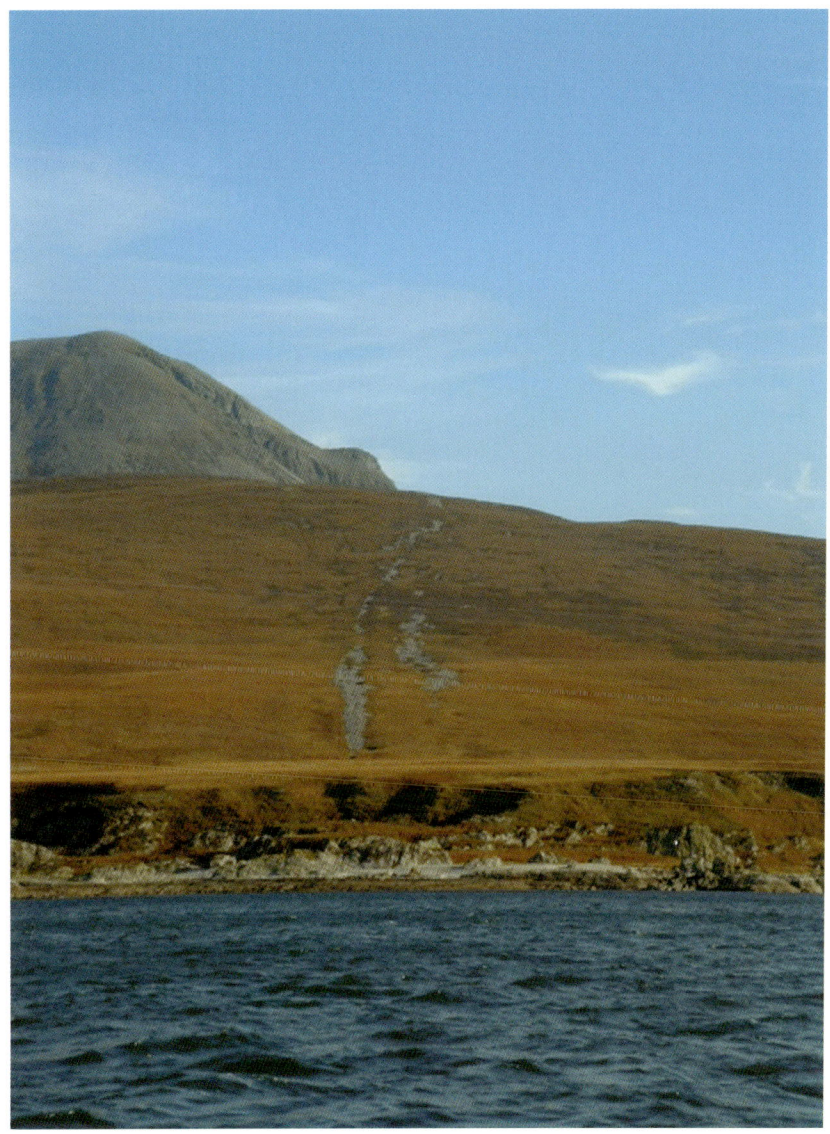

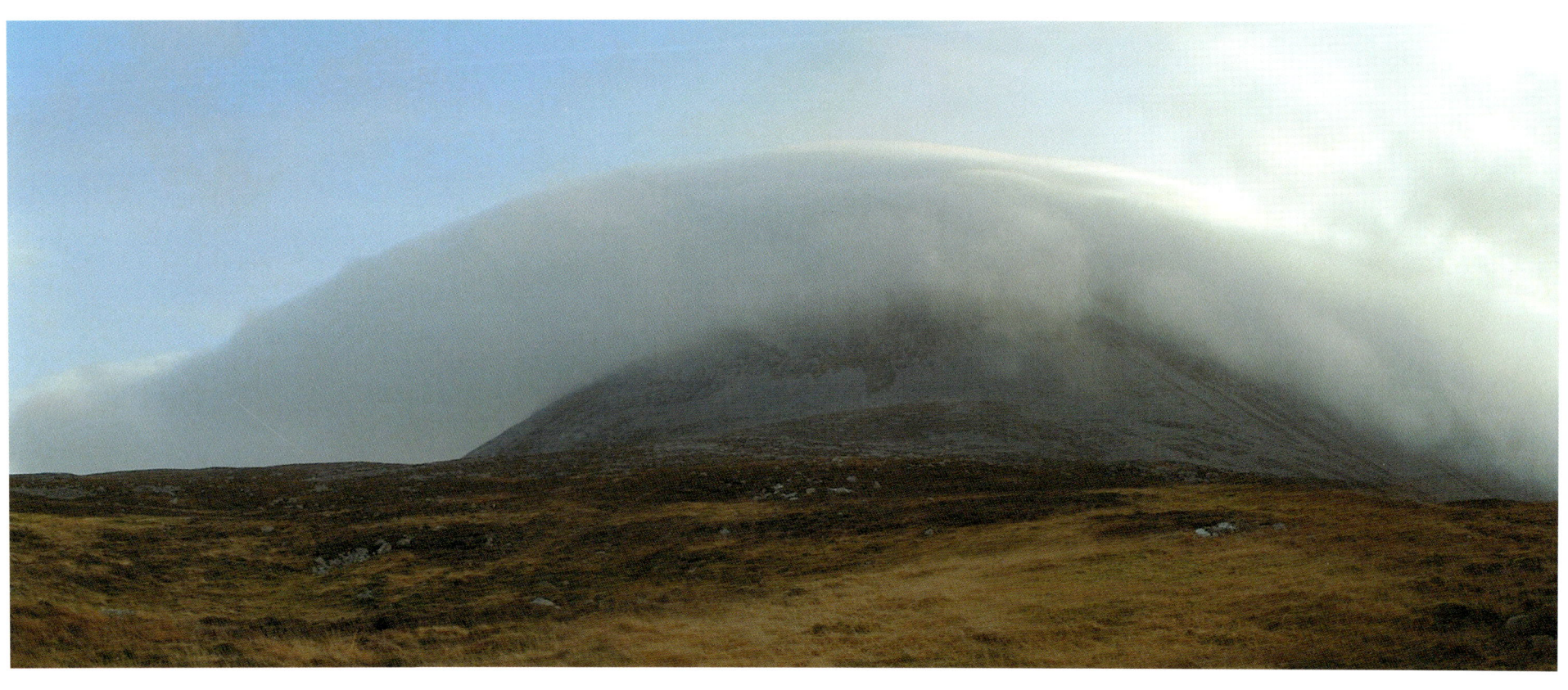